Lecture Notes
in Business Information Processing   120

Series Editors

Wil van der Aalst
  Eindhoven Technical University, The Netherlands
John Mylopoulos
  University of Trento, Italy
Michael Rosemann
  Queensland University of Technology, Brisbane, Qld, Australia
Michael J. Shaw
  University of Illinois, Urbana-Champaign, IL, USA
Clemens Szyperski
  Microsoft Research, Redmond, WA, USA

Lecture Notes
in Business Information Processing 128

Erik Proper
Khaled Gaaloul
Frank Harmsen
Stanisław Wrycza (Eds.)

Practice-Driven Research on Enterprise Transformation

4th Working Conference, PRET 2012
Gdańsk, Poland, June 27, 2012
Proceedings

 Springer

Volume Editors

Erik Proper
PRC Henri Tudor
Luxembourg-Kirchberg, Luxembourg
E-mail: erik.proper@tudor.lu

Khaled Gaaloul
PRC Henri Tudor
Luxembourg-Kirchberg, Luxembourg
E-mail: khaled.gaaloul@tudor.lu

Frank Harmsen
Maastricht University
Maastricht, The Netherlands
E-mail: f.harmsen@maastrichtuniversity.nl

Stanisław Wrycza
University of Gdańsk
Sopot, Poland
E-mail: swrycza@univ.gda.pl

ISSN 1865-1348   e-ISSN 1865-1356
ISBN 978-3-642-31133-8   e-ISBN 978-3-642-31134-5
DOI 10.1007/978-3-642-31134-5
Springer Heidelberg Dordrecht London New York

Library of Congress Control Number: 2012939430

ACM Computing Classification (1998): J.1, H.3.5, H.4, K.6.3

Typesetting: Camera-ready by author, data conversion by Scientific Publishing Services, Chennai, India

Printed on acid-free paper

Springer is part of Springer Science+Business Media (www.springer.com)

Preface

The PRET (Practice-Driven Research on Enterprise Transformation) series of events are set up as one-day events in such a way that they attract an audience from both industry and academia. PRET-4 was organized as the Industrial Track of the CAiSE 2012 conference. For PRET, the CAiSE conference is where it all began. In 2009, the industrial track of CAiSE was organized as PRET-1. Since then, the PRET series have embarked on a journey along several relevant events:

PRET-1 held in 2009 as part of the Conference on Advanced Information Systems Engineering (CAiSE2009) in Amsterdam, The Netherlands

PRET-2 held in 2010 as part of the Enterprise Engineering Week in Delft, The Netherlands, which brought together PRET, the Trends in Enterprise Architecture workshop (TEAR) and the Practice of Enterprise Modelling (PoEM) conference

PRET-3 held in 2011 as part of the IEEE Conference on Commerce and Enterprise (CEC) in Luxembourg

The statement that modern-day enterprises are in a constant state of flux is in 2012 more true than ever. The markets are in a state of confusion and seem to have no direction at all, as they swing back and forth depending on often contradictory signals and economic forecasts. As a consequence, enterprises, be they private businesses, government departments or other organizations, are taking their measures. Restructuring, divesting, improving performance and merging are among the usual transformation activities that enterprises conduct to provide answers to the ever-challenging demands that are put on them. In addition to the tricky economic situation, developments like globalization, rapid technological advancement, ageing and the changing mindset of customers contribute to a situation in which nothing is certain and in which change is the only constant.

PRET approaches these developments and the impact they have on enterprises from a holistic enterprise engineering perspective. Typical questions that are answered in our working conference are:

- How can information technology support and enable enterprise transformation?
- How can enterprises and their transformation be modelled?
- How are information systems transformation and enterprise transformation related?
- How should a transformation be managed?
- How should a transformation be constructed, given the situation at hand?

In the answers, topics are addressed from the people, the process and the technology perspective, thus creating a balanced mix of these three aspects, which are equally important in enterprise transformation.

To foster the much-needed debate between researchers and practitioners, the number of accepted papers at PRET events is purposely kept low. This provides the authors and the audience ample time to engage in discussions about the practical implication of results, and explore the theoretical underpinnings of phenomena observed in practice. This year, the Program Committee selected five excellent papers bridging theory and practice. To foster discussions on the selected papers, 'opponents' were assigned among the authors of different papers, also making sure the discussion focused on the linkage between theory and practice.

Next to the presentations and discussion of the accepted papers, at PRET-4 we also organized a first discussion on the research methodologies to be used for practice-driven research. In several reviews of papers submitted to PRET, this proved to be a contentious topic. The aim of the discussion at PRET-4 was to establish a broader understanding of how to balance the constraints from the commercial reality of the industry projects in which part of our research efforts are to take place, and scientific rigor. The proceedings of PRET-5 will provide a report on the outcomes of this discussion.

We would like to thank the authors, the reviewers, and the audience, for their continuing support in building a bridge between theory and practice. Without them, the PRET series would not have been possible.

April 2012   Erik Proper

Organization

Organizing Committee of PRET-4

Erik Proper	Public Research Centre Henri Tudor, Luxembourg and Radboud University Nijmegen, The Netherlands
Stanislaw Wrycza	University of Gdańsk, Poland
Frank Harmsen	Ernst & Young IT Advisory and Maastricht University, The Netherlands
Khaled Gaaloul	Public Research Centre Henri Tudor, Luxembourg

PRET Steering Committee

Frank Harmsen	Ernst & Young and Maastricht University, The Netherlands
Birgit Hofreiter	Vienna University of Technology, Austria
Erik Proper	Public Research Centre Tudor, Luxembourg and Radboud University Nijmegen, The Netherlands
Stefan Strecker	FernUniversität in Hagen, Germany
José Tribolet	Technical University of Lisbon, Portugal

Standing Program Committee of PRET Events in 2012

Agnes Nakakawa	Radboud University Nijmegen, The Netherlands and Makerere University, Uganda
Alistair Barros	Queensland University of Technology, Australia
Andreas L. Opdahl	University of Bergen, Norway
Anne Persson	University of Skövde, Sweden
Antonia Albani	University of St. Gallen, Switzerland
Barbara Pernici	Politecnico di Milano, Italy
Barbara Weber	University of Innsbruck, Austria
Bas van Gils	BiZZdesign, The Netherlands
Birgit Hofreiter	Vienna University of Technology, Austria
Brian Cameron	Penn State University, USA
Camille Salinesi	University of Paris 1, France
Christian Huemer	Vienna University of Technology, Austria
Christian Schweda	Iteratec Gmbh, Germany

Table of Contents

A Clarification of the Application Concept: The Caixa Geral de Depósitos Case

Pedro Sousa[1,2], Rui Martins[2], and André Sampaio[1]

[1] Link Consulting, Avenida Duque de Ávila, nº23 1000-138 Lisboa, Portugal
[2] Instituto Superior Técnico, Universidade Técnica de Lisboa, Av. Rovisco Pais,
1. 1049-001, Lisboa, Portugal
{pedro.sousa,andre.sampaio}@link.pt, rui.martins@cgd.pt

Abstract. The IT industry is flooded with various terms with more or less obvious meaning; however, in the absence of a strong and precise concept definition, the terms can become the source of confusion and lack of understanding in many of the organizations. Especially terms such as application, information system, and business solution tend to be used indistinctively in various scenarios. The existence of an application/system/solution catalogue is common in many organizations and it is considered a fundamental element that draws attention from the Business, the IS and the IT area. This paper presents a case in which a financial institution considered the need to clarify the Application concept in order to address the problems surrounding an application catalog composed by 500 so called applications. The paper introduces both the taxonomy fundamentals and the recognized benefits. As the result, and considering the coverage and generic nature of the problem, we consider the outcome considerably reusable.

Keywords: Enterprise Architecture, IT Application Concept, Meta Model, IS Taxonomy.

1 The Situation

With over 20.000 employees spread throughout the world and with more than 4 million clients, the CGD (Caixa Geral de Depósitos) is the largest Portuguese financial group, encompassing banks, insurance and medical companies. The SSI (Sogrupo Sistemas de Informação) is the company responsible for supporting all Information Technologies in the group. SSI has approximately 900 workers, being around half external ones, to support all the operation, transformation and management of the IT. The SSI has an ongoing EA (Enterprise Architecture) program which enforces both the descriptive and prescriptive perspective of architecture. It follows TOGAF[3] in its main ideas.

One of the initiatives of this program considers the mapping of all the Information systems in an application catalog supported by the ARIS Platform. At a given point in time the catalogue included more than 500 entries, ranging from small software programs to large banking solutions. However, without considering the effort of an adequate clarification and definition of the notion of Application, the catalogue is far

E. Proper et al. (Eds.): PRET 2012, LNBIP 120, pp. 1–17, 2012.
© Springer-Verlag Berlin Heidelberg 2012

from having the expected benefits, driven by the lack on consensual interpretation of what is an "application" inside the organization.

It is a well-known fact that concept clarification is a complex endeavor. The clarification may encompass both a functional and a constructional description, and in most situations both descriptions are needed. However, the clarification of such key concepts in the IT domain rarely occurs in a systematic manner, simply because professionals of the IT community assume the concept is clear enough. This assumption is further reinforced by the fact that many modelling languages define very precise symbols and rules to represent and relate ill-defined concepts, as happens in some of the most prominent frameworks and modelling languages.

The TOGAF Technical Reference Model[3] considers two types of applications: Infrastructure and Business Applications. However this is a very simple classification schema that does not address fundamental issues in IT management. From an IT and Business alignment point of view, a spreadsheet holding data and business rules is a Business Application, as SAP ERP or any other SW package. But from a management and day to day IT operations they have little in common.

ArchiMate[1,2] refers to the concept of Application Component as self-contained part of a system that encapsulates its contents and exposes its functionality through a set of interfaces. This is true within a large range of scenarios, however it does not help to establish a good enough application concept in order to simplify the communication and actual work within the IT communities.

But the application concept is also a relevant matter within the non-IT communities. In fact, business communities know and use the names of applications in many contexts (e.g. procedures manuals, risk management and so on). This is a problem because it hard-wires a given software element to a set of functionalities and interfaces, removing a degree of freedom from IT management in choosing the best implementation solutions. For example, consider the case where the IT decides to provide access to applications via an intranet, forcing the business to revise documents and procedures. This kind of decisions should not be made more difficult by the naming conventions. The situation is even worse if the application is named after the platform or software packaged used to develop the application.

But there are many more examples where it is fundamental to decouple decisions at the functional level, from the decisions at the IT systems level and also from the IT operation level. The decoupling of such decisions starts with a taxonomy of concepts that must be wide enough to classify a Microsoft Excel program and the Microsoft Excel data file the users create and use, but also the large software packages and software developed in-house.

2   The Project

The project in question had the mission of clarifying the Application concept to key stakeholders across the SSI. The undertaking did not intend to address in excess formal and theory-driven definitions but instead to establish a concept that was useful to the various stakeholders, namely:

- To Business collaborators, that relate to applications that provide services and features that are consumed by the business activities.
- To collaborators that establish the evolution of the features that the Business requires from each of the applications.
- To coworkers whose mission is to construct Information Systems (Systems).
- To employees that maintain the systems operable (Infra-structure).
- To the other employees whose work relates to this concept: Financial Management of the IT; Risk Management; etc.

Even though the results of this project should benefit the above stakeholders, only the IT staff was involved. The project team included 10 members, 2 from the consultants from Link Consulting, and 8 representatives of the different IT areas.

The project was a small one, structured in four half a day workshops with the project team, with some home-work in between. The consulting team had to prepare the sessions and structure their results, and the IT representatives had to validate the results by applying them to real cases in the organization and had to come up with difficulties and suggestions. The project was executed in around 4 calendar weeks, but the overall effort could have been executed in considerably less time.

3   The Approach

The approach taken in the project to clarify the application concept was organized around 3 main stages:

1. **Identification of relevant aspects in concept definition:** In this first stage one identifies the aspects that should be addressed in the definition of the Application concept. Such entailed the different pragmatic ways to make a clear concept.
2. **Identification of relevant perspectives:** In this second stage one identifies the different perspectives that were relevant to the classification of the types of applications.
3. **Concept Representation:** Finally, in this third stage one defines the fundamental views that apply for representation and communication of instances of that concept.

1. Identification of Relevant Aspects in Concepts Definition
The first issue we addressed, to identify the relevant aspects, was to find a metric for the question "how good is good enough" regarding the definition of the application concept. How detailed must such definition be? Here, we adopted the simple rule of thumb: the level of consensus of a given concept is easily established by asking the stakeholders to enumerate the number of instances of the concept in question. Thus,

we believe that the concept of "application" is sufficiently defined if the project team perceives (count) the same number of "applications" that take part of the SSI's IT reality.

In order to establish such consensus, one considers the following aspects to be the ones relevant in the definition of the application concept:

- Lifecycle and the Enumeration – the application's lifecycle, from its birth until it is discontinued, and the identification of the states that are considered in the enumeration task.
- Related Concepts – The clarification of the concepts that are directly related to the concept of "application" is essential to clarify the concept itself because such concepts restrict the application's function and context of existence.
- The Structure – The clarification of the elements that encompass and application is also an important issue in the definition of the concept and in the systematization of its representation.
- The Integrations – The possible integration between the concept's instances was the last considered aspect.

These were the aspects one considered relevant to be clear in order to clearly define the concept of application. Again, each of these aspects should be addressed up to the point where it becomes evident that different people can count the same number of applications in the SSI IT landscape.

2. Identification of Relevant Perspectives

The perspectives that we considered are obvious and common in most frameworks, namely:

- **Business**. The business perspective is the perspective of the end-users, the ones that use IT to execute the inherent function of their activities in the context of the processes and tasks defined in the organization. Naturally we included all support processes and activities – from Human Resources to the development and operationalization of IT.
  This perspective pursues a functional logic, and it is, in its essence, independent of the way IT is implemented and operationalized.
- **Information Systems**. This perspective is focused on the problematic surrounding the construction and maintenance of Information Systems. It remains independent from infra-structure. Consequently, this perspective pursues a constructional logic, and should address the engineering aspects related with the construction and maintenance of the Information Systems.
- **Infra-structure**. This perspective captures issues related to the execution and operation of the Information Systems. The perspective pursues an operational logic, enhancing the necessary operational aspects for the execution of the

Information Systems. Aspects such as business continuity, capacity planning and operational costs over time (disk, cpu and communication) are just examples of the concerns addressed in this perspective.

This means that the application concept that we were looking for must be useful to the issues addressed in each of these perspectives.

3. Concept Representation

Regarding the representation of the application concept, we considered that "applications are systems", and therefore we presume that the key properties and the representation of a System[4] also applies to the application concept. Therefore we adopted as valid the formal descriptions of a system:

- Organic View: Desegregation of overall system into sub-systems grouped by categories.
- Context View: Set of components that are external to the system, which have dependencies with the system.
- Structure View: Representation of the system's components and their dependencies
- Integration View: Representation of the dependencies between the elements of the system and the elements external to the system.

These four views describe the more relevant aspects of the system concept, in a constructional perspective. On the left side of the following image, one can observe a system S01 as the aggregator element of four components. Consider that the circles are concept instances, that the type of the concept is dictated by the color of the circle and that the lines that connect the circles are the relationships between the instances. On the right side of the image the system S01 is an element of the system SA and this one is an element of a Global System.

3.1   Views of a System

In the following text we present the four base views of the S01 system. Take into account that none of the representation intends to define a representation language of SSI. The examples of the views are presented as an example with the sole purpose of facilitating the communication of the message inherent to the application concept.

- Organic View. This view is focused in a hierarchical decomposition, established according to a predefined criterion, which identifies the artifacts in the composition of a system. The Organic View can be represented as follows:
- Context View. This view regards the representation of the elements, external to the system, which have direct dependencies with it. For S01 the Context View presented in Figure 3.

- Structure View. This view regards the representation of the dependencies between the internal elements of the system. The elements are typically organized based on some internal classification. A Structure View of S01 can be represented as in Figure 4.
- Integration View. This view regards the representation of the dependencies between the internal elements of a system and external elements of that system, as presented in Figure 5.

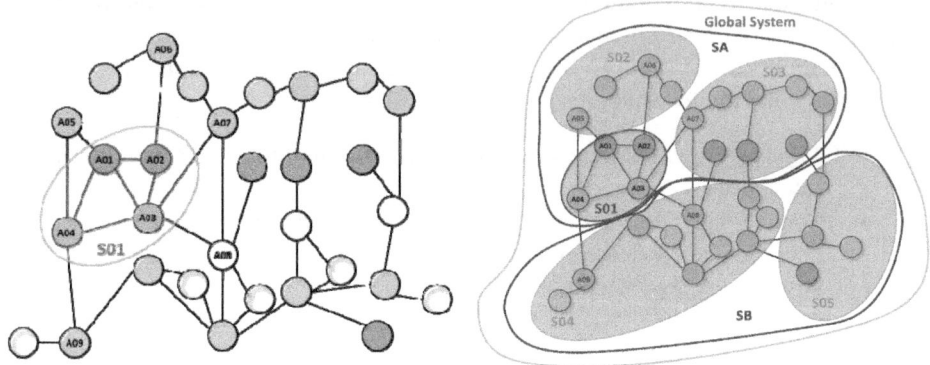

Fig. 1. System S01 as an aggregator element (left) and as an aggregated element (right)

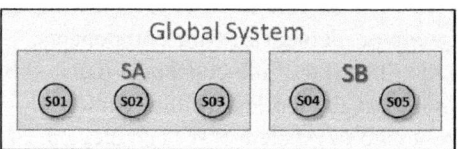

Fig. 2. Organic View with S01

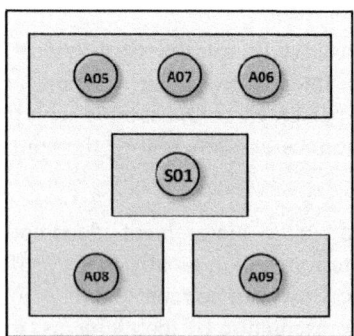

Fig. 3. Context View of S01

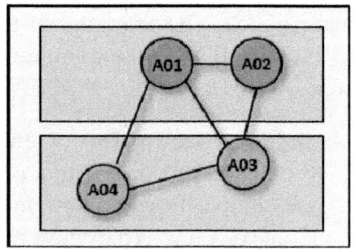

Fig. 4. Structure View of S01

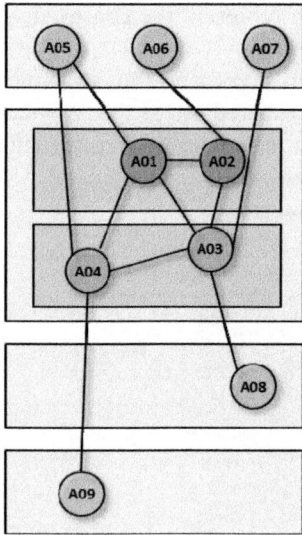

Fig. 5. Integration View of S01

4   The Results

The proposal for the clarification of the application concept is funded on the different needs of the Business, Information Systems and Infra-Structure perspectives. The initial concept was disaggregated into three different ones, each addressing specific logics and purposes:

- The **Solution Concept**, in the Business Perspective.
- The **Application Concept**, in the Information Systems Perspective.
- The **Platform Concept**, in the Infra-structure Perspective.

In Figure 6 we represent these concepts and their dependencies with other concepts that we considered fundamental for the clarification and understanding of the former.

In the Business perspective, the IT is represented by a single concept, the Solution, which provides Functions to the end users – the participants of the Business Processes. We named these functions Business Functions. The Solutions are also associated with Business Areas and to Information Entities. For simplicity purposes, and even thought it was clear that Business.

Processes are related to Business Functions, and Business Functions are related to Solutions, we chose not to depict in the model the Business Function concept, however it is implicit in the relationship between the Business Process and the Solution.

In the Information Systems perspective we considered three base concepts to cover the architectural issues inherent to its construction.

- Applications, which represent the constructive elements that implement and provide Business Functions.
- Repositories, which represent the constructive elements that hold and manage information shared across the Applications.
- Integrations, which represent the constructive elements that enables the integrations between Applications, between Applications and Repositories, and between Repositories.

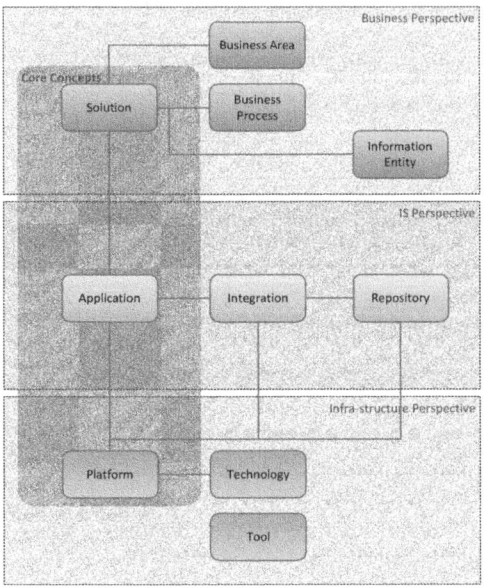

Fig. 6. Concepts by Perspective

Regarding the Infra-structure perspective we considered the Platform concept, which represents the execution environment of the applications, integrations and repositories, or of their components. Such covers the principle that different components of a single application may be executed in different environments (Platforms). A Platform aggregates a series of Technologies used by the Applications during its execution.

After this brief description, we now present a detailed discussion about Solution, Application and Platform concepts.

4.1   The Solution Concept

A Solution is a logical aggregation of Business Functions provided by IT. A Solution has a Functional Responsible, which governs and decides the evolution of such functionalities. A Solution also manages business information that we refer to as Information Entities. The Solution concept does not express any constraint regarding the IS perspective (construction) or Infra-structure (operation).

Solution Lifecycle and Enumeration

The proposed lifecycle for a Solution has four major stages - Conception, Development, Production and Decommissioned - as represented in the following figure.

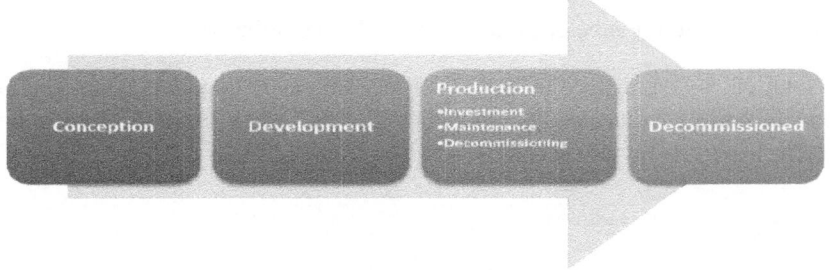

Fig. 7. Solution lifecycle

The Production stage can assume any sub-stage (Investment, Maintenance, and Decommission) in any order. The Investment expresses a phase when the organization is investing in the Solution. The Maintenance dictates that the organization is maintaining the functional and operational level of the Solution. The Decommissioning expresses that the organization is reducing the effort associated with the Solution, and consequently reducing the level of operation.

The lifecycle stages were considered as the basis for the establishment of the enumeration of the concept, allowing the following different counts:

- Number of Solutions in conception;
- Number of Solutions in development;
- Number of Solutions in production.

Solution Related Concepts

As implied in the meta-model presented in Figure 6, there are a few premises inherent to the Solution concept:

- A Solution has at least one association with a Business Process;
- A Solution provides at least a Business Function;
- A Solution has at least one association with an Information Entity.
- A Solution has a Functional Responsible.

The Context View is particularly useful to schematize the relationships of a given Solution; the figure 8 is an example of such.

Solution Structure

A Solution is composed by Sub-Solutions. The decomposition criterion is majorly influenced by the functional complexity, even though it may be reasonable to account for other influences such as security, where one would group the Business Function by access level. A Solution hierarchy is an instrument of structuring of Business Functions and of the way the IT provides services to the Business.

We also identified the following premises surrounding the Sub-Solution notion:

- A Sub-Solution is not subject to Solution enumerations.
- A Sub-Solution has the same lifecycle of the Solution; however they may be in different phases.
- A Sub-Solution belongs to one and only one Solution.

Sub-Solution can be mapped to Business Processes, even though they are not counted individually when inquiring about the amount of Solutions. From an Organic point of view, the Solutions should be placed in a functional hierarchy.

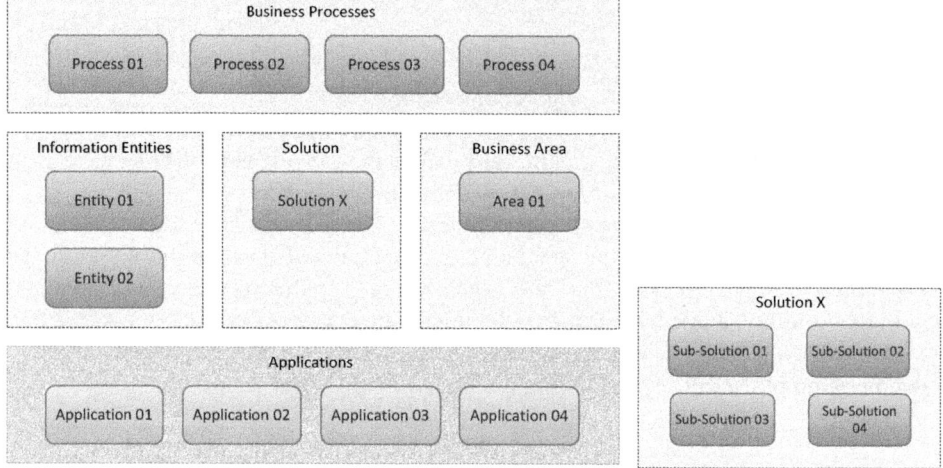

Fig. 8. Context View of a Solution X

Fig. 9. Structure View of a Solution X

Solution Integration

From a Business perspective we can consider the possibility that two Solutions trade information between themselves, and are, by consequence, integrated. However the Integration of Solutions did not come about as a useful constructor and was deemed irrelevant.

4.2   The Application Concept

An Application is an artifact in the Information Systems perspective which implements and/or provides the Business Functions. All Business Functions provided to the end-user by Solutions originate in the Applications. For each Solution there is at least one Application that provides the respective Business Functions. The functions can be implemented by the Application itself, or by another with which the Application is integrated with. Applications may be integrated with other Applications and with Repositories through the Application's components. The components are referenced in the Structure View.

Application Lifecycle and Enumeration
The Application lifecycle is equal to the Solutions lifecycle. However coherence rules between the stages and phases of the concept's lifecycles should be considered. Regarding enumeration, the ways identified to count the applications are equal to the ones of the Solution.

Application Related Concepts
We identified the following premises that are inherent to the Application concept:

- An Application is executed on at least one Platform.
- An Application has at least one associated Solution. The association can be direct or indirect through another Application that provides Business Function implemented by the former. If the Solution has Sub-Solutions the association is established by the Sub-Solutions.
- An Application implements at least one Business Function.
- An Application supports information persistence, either directly through an internal Repository or via integration with an external Repository.
- Applications trade information between themselves and between external Repositories, thus are integrated with other Application and Repositories. Each integration is a relationship between integrated entities and matches an instance of the Integration concept.

Even though a relationship between an Application and another Application or Repositories, is always an Integration, what is relevant to highlight in a constructional logic is the dependency between the integrated entities, and not the integration details. Therefore, an example of an Application Context View can be as follows:

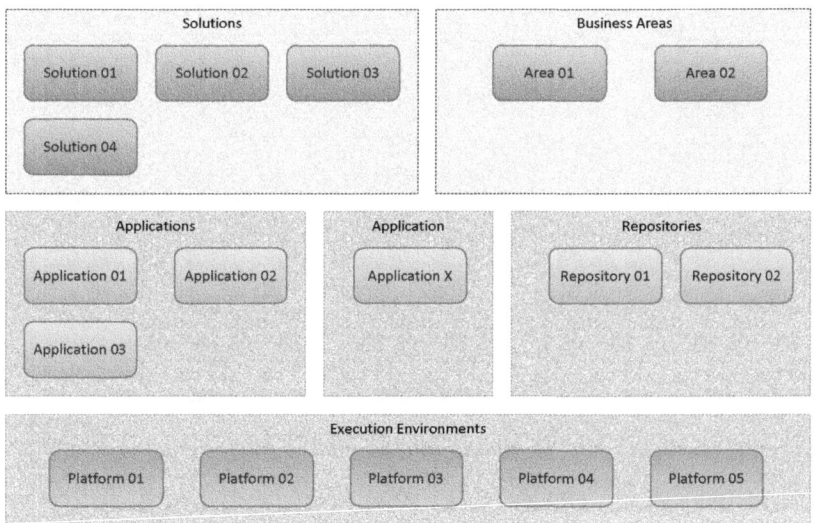

Fig. 10. Application Context View

Application Structure

An application is composed by four types of application components:

- **Presentation Components**, that provide the business functions to the human users. The detail of these components is typically determined by technology issues. Consider, for example, an application that provides an interface view SMS and another via Web. In this scenario one should consider two Presentation Components.
- **Core Components** implement the business functions. Thus different components are mostly justified by functional aspects, although technological considerations may arise, as for example when components require different execution environments.
- **Connectors** that are required to establish the integrations. These connectors are represented whenever a specific parameterization is required for the Integration.
- **Internal Repositories** are the components that ensure the persistence of the information managed by the application, they can relate to databases, system folders or any other way of persistence. An Application can also access information maintained in external Repositories through the Connectors.

Naturally the structure of an Application is not just an enumeration of its components, but also the identification of their interdependencies.

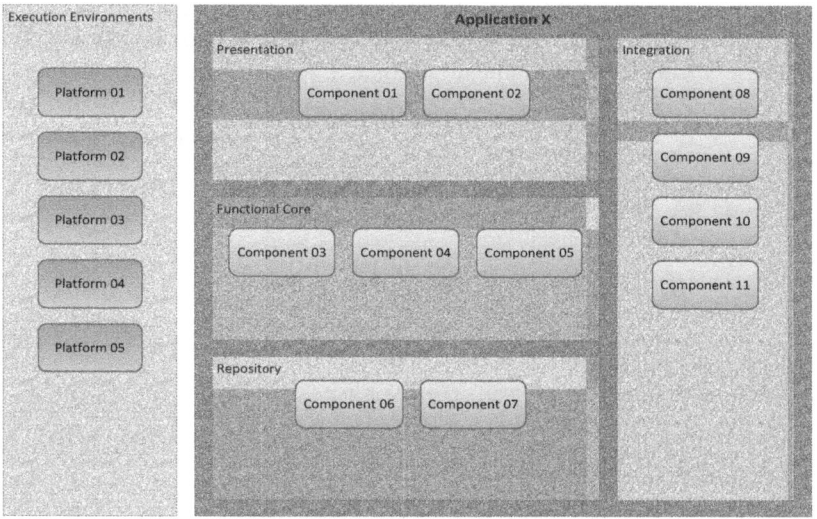

Fig. 11. Application Structure View

All the Application components are associated with execution environments that provide the required resources for their execution. In the majority of cases these environments are Platforms. However in some rare cases, execution environment may not be classified as Platforms.

Consider the example of an ABAP script which is executed in SAP and which extracts data from it to produce a file that is later consumed by a certain Application A developed in dot-Net. If the script exists for the sole purpose of transferring information to Application A, then, even if it is executed in the SAP environment, it is a component of Application A. Namely, it is a Connector of Application A that is executed on SAP. This fact should be registered independently if SAP is classified as a Platform or as an Application.

Thus far we considered that the constituent elements of an Application were "application components", which we have differentiated in four types in conformity to their function in the construction of the application. However there is no limit to the complexity of a component. If we have to represent the structure of the component itself, no matter the type, then we should use the view presented in Figure 11. However, we consider that such need is an exception because we will already be entering in the Engineering domain, instead of Architecture.

Application Integration
Application integration expresses how the application components are integrated with the remaining Applications and Repositories. The following figure is an example of such.

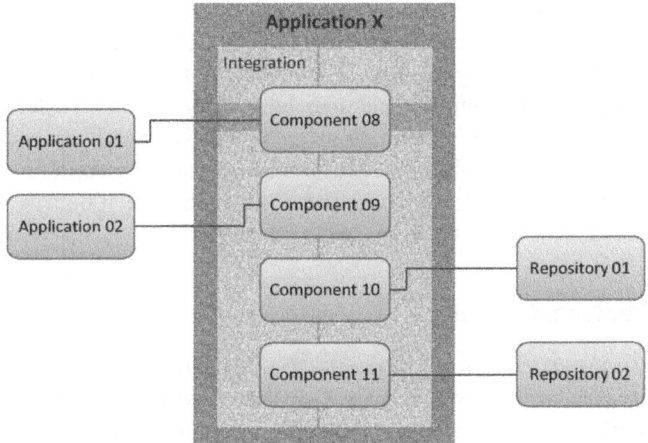

Fig. 12. Application Integration View

A connector can support more than one integration, if its configuration is common to those integrations. Nevertheless a connector is associated with an end-point and therefore two connectors exist for each integration, one for each integrated entity.

This view does not focus on specific integration details. To have a detailed view of a given integration, we can use the structure view applied to Integration, where in addition to both end connectors, the view also presents eventual functional core components holding the integration rules and logic, the data components holding processed flows and logs, and the platforms where previous components execute.

In order to have a better explanation of the Application concept we need to further clarify the related concepts namely, Integration and Repository:

- **The Repository Concept.** From the standpoint of its structure a Repository may be as complex as an Application, taking all kinds of components that an application may have: Presentation Components; Core Components, Connectors and Internal Repositories. A Repository with a back office that allows visual access to the database tables has a Presentation Component. Besides the business information, a Repository can also store information of database accesses, logs for example. Finally, the integration components allow integration with various applications with different technologies and protocols. Therefore, what characterizes a Repository is not only its structure but the fact that its main function is to store information.
- **The Integration Concept.** As previously mentioned, the Integration concept expresses a dependency between two entities and it is materialized in the information flows that those entities exchange. Therefore the Integration doesn't just cover the active elements that establish the communication but the flows that flow through these. Various information flows can be assigned to a single Integration. Integration implies that pair of connectors exists. If there are different ways of communication between two Applications that require various pairs, for example an information transfer via Web-Services and another via File Transfer, then there are two Integrations between the entities. The sole existence of connectors between Applications does not imply the existence of Integration because such would suggest that there was information transfer between them. Take for example three Applications *A*, *B* and *C*, which have connectors to a certain communication platform, but *A* only exchanges information with *B*, and *B* only has trades with *C*. In this case there is no integration between Application *A* and *C*, because there are no flows between them.

4.3   The Platform Concept

A Platform is an execution environment of application components and that may include different forms of Technologies. One can consider various types of Platforms; such classification is influenced by the type/function of components that are executed on each platform. For example, integration Platforms support the execution of connectors by which Applications and Repositories support their integrations.

Platform Lifecycle and Enumeration
The Platform lifecycle is equal to the Solutions and Applications lifecycle. However coherence rules between the stages and phases of the concept's lifecycles should be considered. Regarding enumeration, the ways identified to count the Platforms are equal to the ones of the Applications.

Platform Related Concepts
In terms of relationships with other identified concepts, a Platform has the following premises:

- The execution of a Platform may be supported by another Platform.
- A Platform supports the execution of at least one component, whether it belongs to an Application or a Repository. Such support can be direct or indirect. The later implies that the platform supports the execution of another platform that supports the execution of one or more components.
- A Platform aggregates at least one Technology.

The following depiction is an example of a Platform Context View, through which one can identify the components and Platforms the platform supports, identify the Technologies and have a perception of the influence of the Business Perspective by with the Solutions and respective Applications.

Platform Structure
As stated before, from the standpoint of its structure, a Platform may be as complex as an Application, taking all kinds of components that an Application may have: Presentation Components; Core Components, Connectors and Internal Repositories. Therefore it is possible to consider that the Structure View of the Platform structure is identical the representation of the Application Structure. However, that approach was not perceived to be the most useful to IT from the Infra-structure Perspective. A preferable way to express the structure of a Platform is in terms of the Technologies and Modules it encompasses.

The notion of Technologies included in a Platform concerns with the ability to support the operation of such technology, as for example: Operating Systems, Programing Languages, Communication Protocols, etc. The notion of a Module of a Platform is basically a functional and licensing related concept than a technological one. For example, the different SAP modules are mostly related with functional and licensing concepts. Therefore, the proposed Platform Structure View is as presented in the next figure.

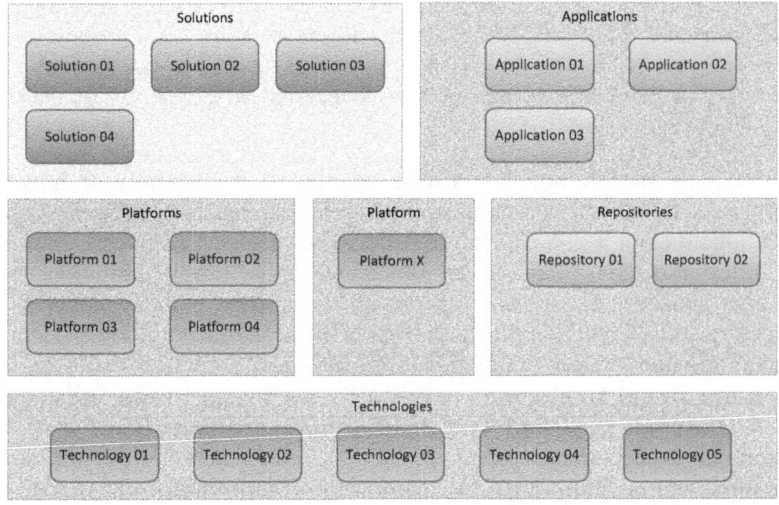

Fig. 13. Context View of the Platform X

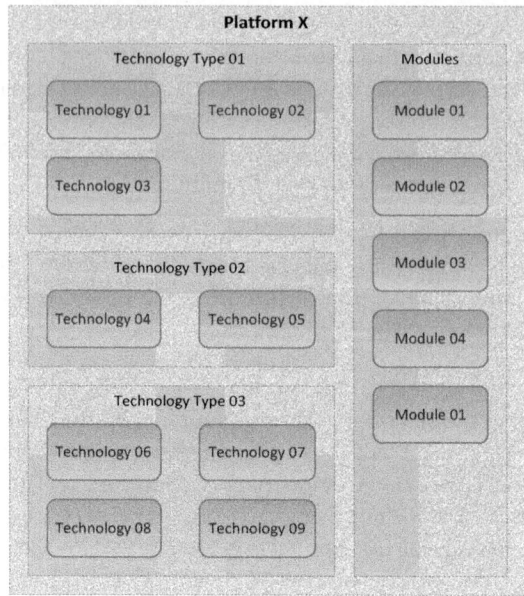

Fig. 14. Platform Structure View

<u>Platform Integration</u>
As happened with the Solutions concept, the notion of platform integration was not considered useful ate this level, and therefore no View was proposed.

5   Reflection

The application concept is a fundamental concept of the organization´s IT. Different communities within an organization use this concept with different meanings, leading to confusion and of overlapping responsibilities. With the proposed solution, Business, IT and Infra-structure communities can use its own concept (Solution, Application and Platform) to manage their concerns independently of the others, as next examples demonstrate:

- Business people are able to manage solutions independently of how they are supported by underlying Applications. For example, if different sub-sets of functionalities of a given Solution need to be managed differently, for example, by different persons, than the Solution can be split into two Solutions, each with its own budget and responsible person. This decision is independent of how the both sub-sets of functionalities are supported at the Information System level, if under the same Application or if in different ones.
- IT can manage Applications mostly driven by a constructive rational, since constructive elements are kept hidden from Business Areas and from the functional aspects that drive them. For example, changing the Applications or Platform that supports a given Solution does not requires changes in the way business refers to IT.

- IT knows that Applications, Integrations and Repositories have organization specific knowledge (code and data) that must be protected and maintain. On the contrary, Platforms are off-the-shelf software. Platforms are replaced with newer versions. Application, Integration and Repository must be migrated whenever the Platforms are replaced.
- Since elements of the Information System layer (Applications, Integrations and Repositories) are mostly customized software, their cost is mostly associated with development and maintenance effort. However, cost structure of software elements of the Infra-Structure layer are mostly associated with licenses costs.
- It is also clear that whenever the organization is acquiring a business package from third parties (for example the SAP ERP for accounting) it is simultaneously acquiring a Solution (once customized), and an Platform, each with specific requirements that must be evaluated. The clarification of these requirements becomes also simpler and more objective.

The proposed concepts were validated with real cases, ranging from simple Microsoft Excel program, to large Data Warehouse systems and to a wide variety of scenarios existing in SSI, either based on acquired packages of develop in house. To conclude, the adoption of the proposed concepts is expected to be a relevant contribution to a better and more rigorous communication among organization communities, enabling by itself a more friendly and productive environment to conduct an Enterprise Architecture initiative.

The results achieved in this project are fully compatible with the notion of "application components" that one can find for example in Archimate. However, the notion of a set of cooperating components, possible executing in multiple platforms, is a relevant concept in the architecture and design of Information Systems and, unfortunately is not considered as such in common modelling notations [1].

References

[1] Lankhorst, M., et al.: Enterprise Architecture at Work: Modeling, Communication and Analysis. Springer, Germany (2005)
[2] Open Group: ArchiMate 1.0 Specification: Technical Standard. Van Haren Publishing, The Netherlands (2009)
[3] Open Group: The Open Group Architectural Framework (TOGAF) - Version 9 Enterprise Edition. Van Haren Publishing, The Netherlands (2009)
[4] Sousa, P., Lima, J., Sampaio, A., Pereira, C.: An Approach for Creating and Managing Enterprise Blueprints: A Case for IT Blueprints. In: Albani, A., Barjis, J., Dietz, J.L.G. (eds.) CIAO! 2009. LNBIP, vol. 34, pp. 70–84. Springer, Heidelberg (2009)

Organizational Configuration Actor Role Modeling Using DEMO

Carlos Páscoa[1,2], David Aveiro[3], and José Tribolet[2,4]

[1] Department of University Education, Portuguese Air Force Academy, Sintra, Portugal
[2] Department of Computer Engineering, Instituto Superior Técnico,
Universidade Técnica de Lisboa, Portugal
[3] Department of Mathematics and Engineering, University of Madeira, Portugal
[4] CODE - Center for Organizational Design & Engineering, INOV,
Rua Alves Redol 9, Lisbon, Portugal
{cjpascoa,daveiro}@gmail.com, jose.tribolet@inesc.pt

Abstract. A certain state of an organization, in its strategic, tactical and operational components results from a combination of elements that makes it a very complex entity. Its components should co-exist in a dynamic and constant balance, whose configuration must have flexible and adaptable reaction mechanisms. As processes increase in complexity, it becomes more difficult to manage an organization, almost in real time, in its many dimensions and configurations. It is therefore essential to identify, given its current complexity, how to guarantee holistic organizational adaptation, agent roles in configuration change and, also, how to design, organize and manage an organization, in the resource domain, considering: i) multiple restrictions; ii) critical needs of real time; iii) various configurations. Using design and action research, our work proposes the concept of organizational configuration, which is managed by the governance sub-system. Based on a *macrogenesis* capability it allows the creatiion and adaptation of transversal transformation mechanisms that, harnessing complexity, are able to maintain the necessary balance to guarantee viability and performance.

Keywords: Organizational Configuration, Actor Role Modeling, Military Organizations, *Microgenesis*, *Macrogenesis*, Flying the Organization.

1   Introduction

Given the increasing organizational complexity, several perspectives have been defined by social scientists, management scientists and engineers that have come together in a shared effort to capture, analyze and understand the multitude of factors that affect the organizational world. Organizations are dynamic systems that run in complex environments and need to react to changes, by increasing its self-awareness and its ability to transform and adapt. Failure to adapt can lead to disruption. Adaptation mechanisms need to consider the wholeness of the organization to maintain its viability and performance.

To steer our research, and due to its similarities to the business organization, we have proposed to use the flying aircraft organization concepts, based on the metaphor

E. Proper et al. (Eds.): PRET 2012, LNBIP 120, pp. 18‑47, 2012.
© Springer-Verlag Berlin Heidelberg 2012

"*Flying the Organization*", proposing to implement, within the business organization, existing aircraft near real time steering concepts. Following design and action research methodologies, we have applied the theory to the Portuguese Air Force.

The document is structured as follows:

- Section 2 introduces the *Flying the Organization* concept, its components, actor roles and the need for near real time steering;
- Section 3 presents the foundations for the Research Context and Research Approach used;
- Section 4 outlines the Aircraft versus Organizational Configurations and their components and similarities, defines an organizational configuration and proposes its definition and high level components.
- Section 5 proposes the organizational configuration actor role modeling, presents examples for its validation and sets the bridge for the Actor Composite Roles proposed in section 2 and the ones found in the research.
- Section 6 concludes and section 7 presents future research recommendations.

2   Flying the Organization

Today, globalization increases the need for constant changes in organizations, made by the need to react to constraints that are imposed but also to the need of steering the organization, using information technologies, in near real time. Thus, the relations between dimensions of an organization need to be dealt with in almost near real time, which calls for adaptability and flexibility.

Reacting to constraints that are constantly changing implies that the organization has a well-defined set of concepts, that are interrelated among each other and also that any change effects are known and reflected through out the whole of the organization.

An organization's ability to implement changes constantly reveals its agility, flexibility and adaptability. Existing national and international contexts impose constant adaptation to different challenges. We argue that failure to adapt can lead to organizational disasters. This requires near real time[1] steering. Therefore the problem

---

[1] A near real-time system is one in which activities completion times, responsiveness, or perceived latency, when measured against wall clock time, are important aspects of system quality. For most of humans, what this means is that the perceived delay between data being available and one's seeing is negligible. The difference among "real time" and "near real time" is both a difference in precision and magnitude. Real-time systems have time constraints that range from microseconds to hours, but those time constraints tend to be fairly precise. Near real time usually implies a narrower range of magnitudes (within human perception tolerances) but typically aren't articulated precisely. In organizations, the definition of "real time" is relative to an organization's critical information needs [14]. Therefore, when applied to the organizational context, and for the purpose of this document, "near real time" means the time that mediates from collecting the external influencer act, and the time of implementing a solution. Naturally, near real time measurement differs in the context of the aircraft (usually seconds or minutes) to the context of the organization (usually days or weeks).

statement is: **organizations do not possess near real time steering mechanisms**. To clarify what we mean by near real time steering mechanisms we start by characterizing the context where they are actually used: the aircraft world.

Flying is exactly the opposite of what is described in the metaphor. Flying is an exact science, requiring precision and accuracy. Flying an aircraft is essentially based on planning, which consists on one building the flight plan and becoming fully aware of all the factors affecting the flight in all its phases, in the context of the flight itself and its surrounding environment. Thus, flying is planning, detail, awareness, precision, learning, monitoring, analysis and reporting in real time, with the aim of *"being ahead of the aircraft"* and being able to predict (and prevent) the existence of exceptions that can result in errors or mistakes. In the flying "business" common errors or mistakes usually cost lives. Flying has proven, over time, that its success lies in some key factors:

- **Culture.** The meticulous preparation of personnel, in terms of operation and maintenance with precise business rules that minimize risk.
- **Mission planning.** Accurate, meticulous and rigorous planning, normally aided by simulators, that results on a precise flight plan that shows where to be at a specific time and what are the planned aircraft status (fuel, altitude, speed, etc.).
- **Configuration selection.** Precise configuration selection down to the detail to achieve a complete controlled internal environment.
- **Real time feedback and control.** Materialized by a cockpit (in the execution phase) which, featuring a set of indicators (including the indication of the position in relation to the ground and to the next waypoint), reveals the state of essential equipment, allowing for situational-awareness and, correction, as necessary.
- **Adjustment mechanisms.** To adjust the various parameters allowing for effective correction and selection of alternatives considered in the planning phase.
- **Debriefing.**

The selection of factors of flight, altitude, speed and fuel are, likewise, essential tools for mission planning. All these mission artifacts are included in the plan to fly the aircraft in a determined **configuration**. If any of the mission planning aspects change during the mission, the aircraft may not be able to attain the desired destination. An engine malfunction, for instance, can cause a route change to an alternate airfield and a need for a configuration change within the mission.

The **near real time** running organization needs to define several configurations, in order to be able to react to adverse or favorable conditions, which can affect its flight plan in a negative or positive way. Therefore, a configuration is a conjunction of aircraft operational and support dimension concepts that permits, in real time, to be acted by crew members that we, now, call actor roles. Based on the aircraft actor roles, Figure 1 presents the **proposed main composite actor roles** whose functions are described next.

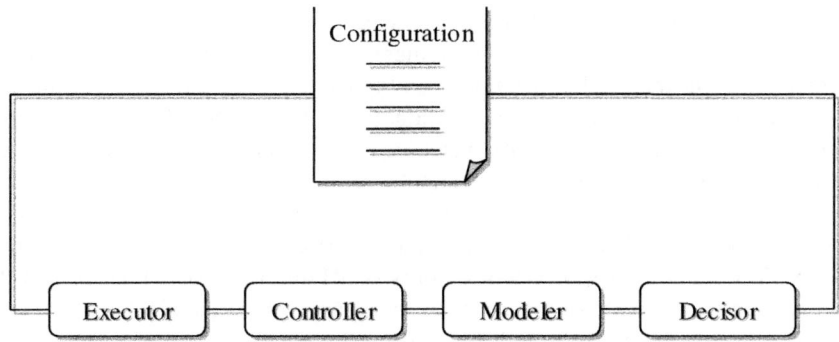

Fig. 1. Real time organization composite actor roles

- The "performer" or "executor", who performs organizational functions using assumptions defined in the configuration rules.
- The "controller" controls the execution, considers whether it meets the configuration conditions by analyzing exceptions and alerts the modeler to the need of setting change, for example, by changing a business rule.
- The "modeler" (or configuration manager), who thinks about the organization and can, due to the execution and the exceptions identified by the controller, change aspects of the configuration or change the configuration itself.
- The "decisor" (or configuration approver), who approves new configurations.

In the discourse of this document **the proposed main composite actor roles** will be studied in order to verify which are present in managing configurations, what functions do they perform and how can they be grouped in composite actor roles.

Near real time steering implies that the configuration, which we now call an **organizational configuration**, is well known and that actors that act upon it know what to change and when. The organizational configuration should allow the following:

- **Fast decisions.** If events appear fast, decisions will have to be fast to prevent that a line of events will be waiting, thus having a negative impact on the organization's performance.
- **Reliable decisions.** Reliability decreases the need for repeated decisions that correct others and therefore has a clear effect on the number of decisions that need to be taken.
- **Accurate decisions.** Precise decisions will have a decisive effect to correct problems and solve dysfunctions.
- **Repeatable decisions.** Situations from the past would have to be recognized in order to identify if the same decisions can be applied with success.

Two examples are in order to clarify the problem: Aircraft O with the mission to fly from point A to point E to deliver T tons of cargo at time TE. The aircraft transports 20 tons of cargo and has 4 crew members, member CM1 to CM4, and 4 engines. To get to point E the organizational configuration entails a strategy of flying at flight level FL at a cruise speed of CS and carrying T tons of fuel for an average fuel consumption of FC tons per hour (all engines). What would happen, during cruise, if the crew finds out that fuel consumption is higher than planned? The organizational counterpart could be exemplified in this situation: Organization O is a company that provides air services. Among its resources are aircraft and helicopters, crew, maintenance and administrative personnel, aeronautical infrastructures (runways, towers, hangars, etc.). The company provides search and rescue alert services 24 hours per day, in 4 distinct locations, and sun rise, sun set alert services in two locations. The number of yearly flying hours is FH and the yearly budget is B. What would happen if, in month M of year Y, the company suffers a budget cut to B-10?

We have stated the problem and clarified what we mean by near real time steering mechanisms characterizing the aircraft world and applying such characterization to the organization world. We claim that, the organization, like the aircraft, needs near real time steering to maintain its viable and performative state. As previously stated, the "flying" concepts can be brought to organizations in general, compared with organization artifacts, improving situational-awareness and, thus, operational value. We propose widespread handling of organizations as aircrafts realizing the intent on the metaphor "Flying the Organization".

Tribolet [1], Magalhães and Tribolet [2] and Páscoa and Tribolet [3] have already proposed to compare flying concepts to organizational concepts, like those proposed by the Business Rules Group (BRG) [4] and Lankhorst et al [5], in such a way that common points can be compared.

3   Research Context and Research Approach

Research can be generally defined as "*an activity that contributes to the understanding of a phenomenon*" [15]. In Design research all or part of the phenomenon may be *created* as opposed to naturally occurring. Knowledge plays a very important part since it allows prediction of the behavior of the phenomenon, as a whole or as a component.

The research was carried within the Enterprise Engineering (EE). Premises of EE proposed in [16] are: i) the enterprise can be viewed as a complex system; ii) the enterprise is to be viewed as a system of processes that can be engineered both individually and holistically; iii) the use of engineering rigor in transforming the enterprise.

The enterprise is viewed as a complex system of processes that can be engineered to accomplish specific organizational objectives. Dietz [7], states that EE is meant the whole body of knowledge regarding the development, implementation and operational use of enterprises, as well as its practical application in engineering projects. The term "engineering" is used in the broad sense, as in mechanical engineering and civil engineering.

Naturally, EE Research (with a perspective of understanding the context of an information system and the processes whereby the system influences and is influenced by its context), borrows standards and methods from Information Systems Research. An interpretive perspective assumes that knowledge about reality is gained through social constructions, such as language, shared meanings, documents, tools and artifacts. It focuses on the complexity of human sense–making, and attempts to understand phenomena through the meanings that people assign to them.

Therefore, *"one can conclude that information systems engineering is about the design and modeling of systems for information processing in an organizational context requiring to be grounded not only on technological requirements but also on requirements taken from the organizational, social and human sciences"* [17].

Hevner et al [18] affirm that two paradigms characterize much of the research in the information systems discipline: behavioral science and design science. The behavioral-science paradigm seeks to develop and verify theories that explain or predict human or organizational behavior. The design-science paradigm seeks to extend the boundaries of human and organizational capabilities by creating new and innovative artifacts.

Both paradigms are foundational to the Information Systems (IS) discipline, positioned as it is at the confluence of people, organizations, and technology. The general methodology of design research requires knowledge and understanding of a problem domain. Its solution is achieved by a process of suggestion (tentative design) that culminates by the building and application of the designed artifact. In order to assess how the design artifact will be presented under the design research standards, seven guidelines (for understanding, executing, and evaluating the research) are proposed:

- *Guideline 1 –* **Awareness of the Problem.** Awareness of an interesting problem may come from multiple sources. The output of this phase is a Proposal, formal or informal, for a new research effort.
- *Guideline 2 –* **Suggestion and Tentative Design of an Artifact**. Design research must produce an idea and tentative design for a viable artifact in the form of a construct, a model, a method or an instantiation.
- *Guideline 3 –* **Development**: The Tentative Design is implemented in this phase. The objective is to develop technology-based solutions to important and relevant business problems. A combination of technology-based artifacts, organization-based artifacts, and people-based artifacts are necessary to address such issues.
- *Guideline 4 –* **Evaluation**: Once constructed, the artifact should be evaluated according to criteria that are always implicit and frequently made explicit in the Proposal (Awareness of Problem phase). The utility, quality, and efficacy of a design artifact must be rigorously demonstrated via well-executed evaluation methods. To evaluate the utility of the design artifact we use two techniques from Hevner's [18] descriptive evaluation method: *"Informed Argument – Use information from other relevant research work to build a convincing argument for the artifact's utility"* and *"Scenarios – Construct detailed scenarios around the artifact to demonstrate its utility"*. Building scenarios and test them, based on premises, also falls into the field of Action Research.
- *Guideline 5 –* **Conclusion and Research Contributions**. Effective design research must provide clear and verifiable contributions in the areas of the design artifact, design foundations, and/or design methodologies. The ultimate assessment for any research is *"What are the new and interesting contributions?"*.

- *Guideline 6* – **Research Rigor**. Design research artifacts rely upon the application of rigorous methods in both the construction and evaluation of the design artifact.
- *Guideline 7* – **Communication of Research**. Design research must be presented effectively both to technology-oriented as well as management-oriented audiences.

This research proposes an organization metaphor[2] as a conceptual framework. The organization has a reason to exist, which gives birth to its mission. The organization has a business model, a mission, a structure, influencers, ends, means (business processes use all of these) that we intend, in the discourse of this work, to classify in the organizational configuration concept.

4   Aircraft versus Organizational Configurations

4.1   Aircraft Configuration

Aircraft designs are the result of the integration of several systems (structure, propulsion, electrical, navigational, etc.) that function in an orchestrated manner in order to maintain its viability and performance. In an aircraft, the basic thing that should be assured is that it can fly safely. However, there are things that can vary based on what the aircraft is supposed to do. Candidate configurations are proposed with a decision on the type of payload and "the mission" the airplane is supposed to carry out with this payload, expressed generally in terms of knowing the aircraft, its ability to perform in certain conditions and the external environment rules: What are the aircraft components? What can it carry? How far can it go? How fast can it fly? What is the fuel consumption? How high in altitude can he fly? What are the requirements for operation (runway length, maneuvering, acceleration, stop time, etc.)? What are the limitations for a specific condition? What are the regulations it should obey?

To exemplify how aircraft configurations work we present an example: take a commercial aircraft "A" that has 100 tons of payload (fuel, persons and cargo). Its maximum fuel load is 70 tons (which will enable 10 hours of flight). Its cargo compartment is tailored for three possible events: maximum passenger (200 seats), maximum cargo (30 tons) or a combo of passenger and cargo, that will allow 200 passengers.

Depending on the "mission", which configures the distance to be flown, altitude, fuel consumption and the type of payload, the aircraft can have distinct configurations. Table 1 presents some of the possible configurations.

---

[2] From Greek metafo'ra which means to transfer from one place to another (Royal School of Library and Information Science, 2010). Knowles & Moon [19] define a metaphor as: *"the use of language to refer to something other than what it was originally applied to, or what it 'literally' means, in order to suggest some resemblance or make a connection between the two things"*. Lakoff & Johnson [20] defend that the human being not only talks metaphorically much of the time, but that may also think metaphorically much of the time. Morgan & Smircich [21] citing Brown [22], Morgan [23] and Schon [24], defend that is through the use of metaphors *"that scientists seek to create knowledge about the world"*.

Table 1. Aircraft Possible Configurations example

Mission	Configuration
Fly from Lisbon to New York taking 200 passengers	Maximum range, maximum passenger: the airplane will be configured with 70 tons of fuel and 200 seats in the cargo compartment.
Fly from Lisbon to Amsterdam, taking 100 passengers and cargo	Medium range, medium passenger: the airplane will be configured with 30 tons of fuel and 100 seats in the cargo compartment. The rest will be available to cargo.
Fly from Lisbon to Amsterdam, taking cargo	Medium range, maximum cargo: the airplane will be configured with 30 tons of fuel and no seats in the cargo compartment.

From the previous paragraphs and the examples given, we can conclude that an aircraft configuration is a set of components that are combined in an optimal manner to perform the mission and achieve its end state.

Like an aircraft, an organization also has a set of components that have to be considered, in possible combinations to perform its mission and achieve its end state, which we claim to be an organizational configuration.

4.2   Organizational Configuration

Upon stating the need for near real time steering, using the metaphor *flying the organization* and bringing principles of an aircraft configuration into an organizational configuration, we explained what a configuration is and coined its applicability in the organizational world. As an analogy to the aircraft world, we claimed that a near real time organization needs configurations to clearly identify: i) WHAT is on the configuration; ii) WHO manages the configuration; iii) WHEN is the configuration managed.

Applying the aircraft example to the organization, we define an Organizational Configuration **as a *set of organizational artifacts that drive its means, in an optimal and orchestrated manner, in order to achieve its ends*.**

On an aircraft the crew knows the configuration components, which we call the WHAT, WHO manages the configuration (that is, WHO manages the WHAT) and WHEN to manage (that is, WHEN does the WHO manage the WHAT). Therefore, related to organizational configuration concept, we propose to devise our contribution in three components: the *What*, the *Who* and the *When*, as shown in Figure 2.

- On the WHAT component we state the question: What are the concepts that compose the Organizational Configuration?
- On the WHO component we state the question: Which actor roles contribute to the Organizational Configuration management?
- On the WHEN component we state the question: When is the Organizational Configuration managed?

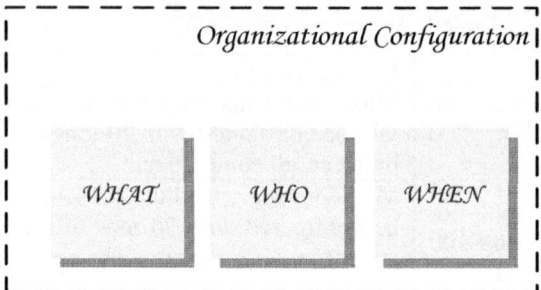

Fig. 2. Organizational Configuration components

As a result of the three components, a new question arose: how do they relate in terms of what happens to the WHAT as a consequence of the WHO and the WHEN and how can they be measured against or, in other words, what would be the appropriate criteria parameters that would allow to verify and validate the advantages of the proposed solution?

Again, taking by example what happens in the aircraft, we made the following statements: i) the aircraft configuration (the WHAT) serves as a basis for conducting the flight and evaluate anything that happens in terms of what is affected in the wholeness of the configuration; ii) the aircraft present and future flying conditions are constantly monitored and evaluated by the crew (the WHO) that takes the convenient actions to alter the configuration when something is affecting or is thought to affect it (the WHEN).

We defined the organization configuration map (the WHAT) divided on 3 main areas: BEING, BECOMING and BEHAVING. BEING defines the identity of the organization, like a human being and identifies its business model, structure, governance and resources. BECOMING defines what the organization wants to be in the future and identifies its ends, means, influencers, business processes, assessment and potential impact. To further clarify organizational options and provide the bridge from planning to execution, the strategy map/balanced scorecard, context diagram and activity plan concepts were added. BEHAVING identifies how the organization is doing in reaching its future state. It encompasses the concepts simulator, dashboard (cockpit) and adjustment mechanisms. **However, due to its extent, the WHAT component will not be further developed in this document**.

To characterize the WHO and WHEN, we took the (re)Generation, Operationalization and Discontinuation (G.O.D.) organization [6] as a basis to define a Design & Engineering Methodology for Organizations (DEMO) [7; 8; 9] artifact that identifies the actor roles involved in managing the organizational configuration.

5   Configuration Actor Role Modeling Using DEMO

Section 4 defined the elements that compose an organizational configuration map that we stated to be the WHAT component (which is not a part of this document). The real time organization is actually working on rules set for a specific configuration.

This section describes the formulation for the WHO and the WHEN components of the organizational configuration that, in our view, establishes its governance sub-system. For consistency sake and future use, the DEMO related material is presented in this section.

The issue of continuously modeling change, neglected from Organizational Self Awareness (OSA) and Organizational Design Engineering (ODE), can be emphasized in the way that "making knowledge about the history of organizational change and lessons learned explicit in models will aid future change decisions taken by the organizational engineers" [6].

An effective diagnosis of dysfunctions needs an up to date picture of organizational reality, as well as relevant historical information of this same reality. To solve this problem, this aspect of continuously modeling change needs to be addressed. [6] proposed a novel notion of the function perspective of an organization which helped to frame the solution to this problem. The function perspective aggregates four perspectives of an organization system.

- The construction perspective the concerns are centered with the concrete realization of the system in its component parts, such as actor roles and transaction kinds that specify the interaction between such roles.
- The behavior perspective is only concerned with the external manifestation of operation of the organization, regardless of its internal construction[3].
- The resilience perspective focuses on awareness of what is considered to be normal and accepted behavior of the organization so that it remains viable. Viability has to be systematized in a set of **norms** describing certain properties relating to the organization's operation and accepted values for such properties. Deviations in such accepted values imply a state of dysfunction which can compromise the viability of the organization. Central to this perspective, are resilience strategies which are activated to address the expected exceptions causing dysfunctions. If successful, these strategies will cease the observed dysfunctions. If they are unsuccessful, *microgenesis* dynamics have to come into play.
- The *microgenesis* perspective tells us that one has to first diagnose unexpected exceptions causing dysfunctions which were not successfully handled by resilience dynamics. Then, a creative process comes into action which will change the construction of the organization to solve or circumvent the (previously unexpected) exceptions causing dysfunctions. This solving consists in the generation, operationalization and/or discontinuation of appropriate and needed Organizational Artifacts (OA).

One of possible solutions is the *microgenesis* and *autopoesis* constant monitoring and changing of processes proposed by [6] in the (re)G.O.D. theory. However, the notion of the (re) G.O.D. Organization allows handling dysfunctions one by one allowing the organization to create self-awareness and a databank of factual knowledge, is, in our

---

[3] These construction and behavior perspectives have been addressed systematically and thoroughly in [7]. Aveiro [6] focused is on the other two perspectives that he considered to be part of his proposal for the function perspective of an organization.

view, although an essential base, a reactive approach to the whole of the organization. In fact, we defend that organizations need holistic pro-active approaches to find their way through the path of global competitiveness.

Naturally, the constant monitoring of the organization can also be seen as a business process of self-awareness that has, as a final objective, to catch exceptions, to identify them and to solve them changing the organization along the process.

In this section, using concepts from Ψ-theory and DEMO as a base, we systematically delineate the path from our research problem to a design artifact that constitutes our solution to model the organizational configuration actor roles. In short, we propose that organizations should explicitly design and deploy their actor roles which systematize, respectively, resilience and *macrogenesis* dynamics.

Dysfunctions that compromise an organization's viability will have a cause which may be expected or unexpected. If the cause is an expected exception, certain resilience strategies may already exist that can be activated by the control organization to eliminate or circumvent such dysfunctions. As stated by Aveiro [6], if the cause is an unexpected exception, the G.O.D. organization will intervene to diagnose the cause. The difference to the organizational configuration is that, after diagnosis, it will Generate, Operationalize and/or Discontinue parts of the total organization – which may include the wholeness of the organization, executing, in this case, what we call *macrogenesis* dynamics to eliminate dysfunctions.

We apply the DEMO methodology and some relevant theoretical concepts underlying it to specify and make explicit these actor roles in managing and changing configurations.

We adopt Aveiro's [6] statement that argues that when one needs to decide on changing norms or resilience strategies it will be useful to know how a certain resilience strategy has performed in the past.

We propose the notion of organizational configuration as corresponding to the organization system's composition, structure and production while maintaining a viable and performative state. These are the properties of the adopted notion of an organization system: the ontological. In a certain point in time, a set of representations (like a set of DEMO diagrams and tables) will denote a certain state of this organizational self, e.g., the current state of organizational reality. An organizational configuration specifies the generic *macrogenesis* dynamics that occurs in every organization and keeps information of the current and past states of the organizational self.

In other words, state information of all OAs that constitute an organization and relationships among them is formally managed by the G.O.D. organization. From this information we can coherently derive representations that denote organizational reality, both in its current and past states. Under these circumstances, we achieve one of the aims of OSA: to provide a coherent and consistent history of organizational change up to its current state.

In a nutshell, our solution proposal makes it possible that, besides the history of the operation of an organization – currently captured in DEMO models – we can also have the history of an organization's changes, essential information for aiding the process of change itself and do it in a macro way, which is transversally to the wholeness of the organization system.

Aveiro [6] recalled, in his research problem, the finding that, in OE, there is an absence of concepts and a method for explicit capture and management of information of exceptions and their handling, including the design, operationalization and/or discontinuation of OA to solve dysfunctions. In other words, unexpected exceptions need to be diagnosed so that concrete and new organizational change can be realized.

Aveiro [6], with the intent to clarify the Notion of Organizational Self-Awareness, proposes a definition of what constitutes an organization system and its ontological model which he named the organizational self state (of an organization system's composition, structure and production).

From Dietz [8], the formal definition of the ontological model of a world is: "*the specification of its state space and its process space*", both expressed in business rules. The state space means a set of allowed or lawful states within the existence of defined laws. Process space devises the set of allowed or lawful sequences of events within the occurrence laws (the set of event types of which instances may occur in the world).

Also from Dietz [9], we find that in the Ψ-theory based DEMO methodology, four aspect models of the complete ontological model of an organization are distinguished. The Construction Model (CM) specifies the construction of the organization: the actor roles in the composition and the environment, as well as the transaction kinds in which they are involved.

The Process Model (PM) specifies the state space and the transition space of the C-world. The State Model (SM) specifies the state space and the transition space of the P-world. The Action Model (AM) consists of the action rules that serve as guidelines for the actor roles in the composition of the organization.

Aveiro [6] also defends that in Dietz [7] it is considered that the notion of system state is ambiguous, because changes in the composition or structure of a system may also be considered as state changes. The current notions of coordination and production worlds of an organization "O" provided in DEMO do not address the issue of changes in the state of the composition, structure and production of the organization system. They only address changes in the state of its operation. These worlds focus on what "O" produces to its environment and coordination dynamics that occur for such production.

In complex adaptive systems literature we find the concept of dynamic models as being models with changing configurations. The purpose in constructing a dynamic model is to find unchanging laws that generate the changing configurations. These laws correspond roughly to the rules of a game. In a game, the rules say how the configurations (states) change as different moves are made; the players affect the course of the game by choosing moves [6] citing [10;11].

We reiterate that one of the aims of our research is to specify *macrogenesis* dynamics which change the organizational self. In this manner we can enable continuous synchronization of organizational reality with its (conceptual) ontological model and representation, realizing OSA.

Aveiro [6] applied DEMO to specify the G.O.D. Organization (GO) that he considers to exist in every organization. Namely he specified the GO's: i) construction; ii) state; iii) process; iv) action spaces, e.g., the organization artifacts (or rules/laws) governing *microgenesis* in terms of, respectively: i) actor roles allowed to conduct *microgenesis* dynamics and interactions between them by certain allowed transactions; ii) allowed facts and results that characterize the state of the GO's world;

iii) allowed events that characterize state changes of this same world; iv) action rules guiding *microgenesis* dynamics.

Organization artifacts constituting the organizational self are arranged in a certain manner as to specify all the spaces (state, process, action and construction) of an organization's world, e.g., they have to obey certain rules of arrangement between them. We will call the conceptualization of these rules as the ontological meta model of the world. The ontological meta-model is the conceptualization of the organization space. By organization space we understand the set of allowed organization artifacts. It is specified by the organization artifact base and organization artifact laws. The organization artifact base is the set of organization artifact kinds of which instances, called organization artifacts. We proposed to use DEMO to characterize the organizational configuration governance sub-system, that is, the WHO that acts on the WHAT and WHEN.

In section 5.1, we identify the organizational actor roles that closely related to establishing an organizational configuration and we apply DEMO to specify the Actor Role Organization (governance sub-system). The Actor Role Organization's ontological model is the specification of a generic pattern considered to exist in every organization and responsible for controlling its viability, e.g., realizing macro, pro-active, resilience dynamics.

In section 5.2, we present two examples of actor role actions on the WHAT validating the pro-active way of changing the organization as a whole, introducing the concept of macro change that we call *macrogenesis*.

In section 5.3, we compare the composite actor roles found with the ones presented in section 2 and identify a relation between them, depending on the organization nature.

5.1   Actor Role Organization Modeling

The main focus of our research is the change of the organizational wholeness self to solve dysfunctions caused by unexpected exceptions in a pro active way. We consider that this wholeness change, with a transversal effect, can be called a *macrogenesis* kind of change.

Before we focused on how to precisely and coherently specify the actor role in developing, implementing and changing configurations, providing a *macrogenesis* kind of change (considering the system wholeness), we learned from [6] how to focus on how to precisely and coherently specify the resilience kind of change. *Microgenesis* change starts in a particular context in resilience dynamics, namely, when a certain dysfunction cannot be solved by any existing resilience strategy.

Apparently, the relevant unit of service of *organizational configuration* is the target organization's *modus operandis* for some period. In the case description this notion was already designated by "Organizational Configuration". The Organizational Configuration is a space-time notion, like e.g. the loan of a book from a library, or the rental of a hotel room, as indicated by [12]. In this context, we argue that *an organizational configuration* sets out the best organizational BEING, BECOMING and BEHAVING, operating for any organization that can define the configuration components.

To define an organizational configuration, actor roles take the organization as a system, with sub-systems, working with and for other systems, subject to the environment (coming from other systems), with self-regulation systems. The organizational configuration should be developed at the strategic level of the organization, in direct coordination with other levels, by taking each element of the configuration and studying the relations between them and asserting if the configuration is viable and able to maintain the expected performance. To assert if the configuration is viable, the organization should use a database of knowledge of events that occurred in the past and constitute organizational memory. Simulators can also be used to test if the different aspects of the organization are viable as a whole. Naturally, common sense and reaching a coordinated agreement is also a way to attest the organizational configuration viability and performance ability.

We assume that there is an organizational configuration running on any organization (in fact we can assume that every organization has a running organizational configuration, although, it may not be aware of it). Once the configuration is set and running we identify one transaction kind, which we will call *influencer entity monitoring* (T-01), executed by the actor role A-01 *influencer entity monitor* which scans the internal and external facts in the organization and, after registering the corresponding date/time stamp decides if a particular fact has impact in the existing *organizational configuration*.

When the *influencer entity monitor* decides that a fact could be relevant to the organizational configuration he starts the transaction T-02 *influencer fact specification*, performed by the actor role A-02 *influencer fact specifier* whom starts the transactions T-03 *influencer fact categorization*, T-04 *influencer fact description* and T-05 *influencer fact naming*. These transactions intend to fully characterize the influencer fact and are performed respectively by the actor roles A-03 *influencer fact categorizer*, A-04 *influencer fact descriptor* and A-05 *influencer fact namer*. A discussion could be performed, if the situation permits, between A-04 and A-05 in order to proper name and describe the influencer fact.

After the fact has been specified the actor role A-01 calls a new transaction T-06 *organizational governance process execution* which is performed by the actor role A-06 *organizational governance process executor*. The objective of this transaction is to start the process of analyzing the transversal impact of the influencer fact on the existing organizational configuration and to recommend changes, if necessary, in order to recommend pro-active changes to allow rapid adaptation to the influencer fact.

Actor role A-06 calls the transaction T-07 *impact specification* which is done by actor role A-07 *impact specifier* which, in turn, calls transaction T-08 *impact categorization* which is done by actor role A-08 *impact categorizer*. The impact category classifies the influencer fact in the SWOT universe identifying its scope within the strength, weakness, opportunity and threat. The influencer fact can be categorized in more than one category. After the *impact categorization* is completed actor role A-06 calls the transaction T-09 *impact description* done by actor role A-09 *impact descriptor* that produces, on a free text format, a description of the influencer impact on the organizational configuration.

Once the *impact categorization* has been completed, A-06 calls the transaction T-10 *organizational configuration change proposal*, performed by actor role A-10 *organizational configuration change proposer* which will start the process of identifying, in a transversal manner, the impact of the influencer fact in the organizational objectives, and build a proposal with the organizational configuration changes necessary to solve the dysfunction considering the organization's wholeness. Actor role A-10 is actually assessing the changes that the organization configuration will need in order to transversally react and adapt to the influencer fact.

Reaction and adaptation to the new reality occurs in the form of maintaining or changing the organizational flight plan destination, that is, the desired end state that, in the organizational configuration context takes the form of Ends that usually are business goals and objectives (that we call goals and sub-goals).

Not all the forms of reaction actually mean that the organization has to change its destination. In some cases, and according to Aveiro's G.O.D. theory [6], the impact can be solved by activating a resilience strategy or by changing a control parameter with minor or no impact on the organizational configuration. Other reaction forms include the generation or discontinuation of organizational artifact bundles or the generation or discontinuation of resource bundles. The difference to G.O.D. theory is that the form of reaction and adaptation takes in consideration the wholeness of the organization materialized in an organizational configuration. This is the reason why we claim that the macro change on the wholeness of the organization configuration can be considered *macrogenesis*.

Other difference to the G.O.D. theory is that we can not assume that the generation will happen immediately after it has been ordered. Generation, operationalization and discontinuation of organizational artifacts are implemented by cooperative organizational actions (called programs or projects[4] – outside the scope of this work) that take time. The notion of time, on this context, can cause that influencer fact may impact the generation of an organizational artifact that is not yet completed and cause its cancellation. Ontologically, if a generated organizational artifact was not yet operationalized, it could not be discontinued. Therefore, the notion of *cancellation* is needed to explain that, at Time T, the generation can be stopped.

The *organization configuration proposal* is actually a course of action composed of several *organizational configuration elements*, representing strategy, which goes through 3 possible states: i) creation of a new organizational element; ii) discontinuation of an organizational element; iii) cancellation of an organizational element (that was being operationalized).

In this context, to assess the form of reaction most adequate to the influencer fact, and due to the ontologic need for differentiation between actions, actor role A-10 calls transaction T-11 *organizational configuration element proposal*, performed by actor role A-11 *organizational configuration element creation proposer*.

To proper characterize the *organizational configuration element creation proposal* actor role T-11 calls transaction T-12 *organizational configuration element categorization*, performed by actor role A-12 *organizational configuration element categorizer*. Categorization encompasses the possibilities precluded in the G.O.D. theory: resilience strategy, *control parameter change, organizational artifact bundle generation, organizational artifact bundle discontinuation, organizational resource bundle generation* and *resource bundle discontinuator* and adds the cancellation possibility for each. The options in the *organizational configuration element categorization* can have the form of: resilience *strategy {activation, discontinuation and cancellation}, control parameter change, organizational artifact bundle*

---

[4] Some authors defend that a program comprehends one or more projects.

{generation, discontinuation and cancellation}, and *resource bundle {generation, discontinuation and cancellation}*.

All *organizational configuration elements categories* and the corresponding *states* are stored as a single organizational artifact repository. After the *organizational configuration element categorization* has been completed, with the intent of adding a description, an impact description and to get decisor feedback, T-11 calls the transactions:

– T-13 organizational configuration element descriptor, performed by actor role A-13 organizational configuration element descriptor.
– T-14 *organizational configuration element goal impact*, performed by actor role A-14 organizational configuration element goal *impactor*.
– T-15 *organizational configuration element goal impact description*, performed by actor role A-15 organizational configuration element goal impact descriptor and,
– T-16 organizational configuration element decisor feedback, performed by actor role A-16 organizational configuration element decisor. This transaction intends to verify if the decisor, which is normally at an intermediate level agrees with the *organizational element proposal*.

These actor roles assess the influencer impact and propose several strategies (*organizational configuration element*), with impact on goals and return the impact assessment to A-10, which, in turn, builds the overall assessment, in form of a *organizational configuration change proposal*, for the several options (*organizational configuration element*) that can affect the organizational configuration. The *organizational configuration change proposal* can consider one *organizational configuration element* or a composition of several *organizational configuration elements*.

Additionally A-10 devises an implementation (*TO BE*) by adding the necessary information and actions that will need to be taken in order to implement the proposed solution (*organizational configuration change proposal*).

Once the TO BE *organizational configuration plan proposal* is completed, A-10 calls the transaction T-17 *TO BE organizational configuration change proposal approval*, performed by actor role A-17 *TO BE organizational configuration change proposal approver*.

Once the *TO BE organizational configuration plan proposal approval* is completed, A-17 calls the transaction T-19 *TO BE organizational configuration implementation*, performed by A-19 *TO BE organizational configuration implementer*, which, in turn calls the transaction T-19 *organizational artifact element state change*, performed by actor role A19 *organizational artifact element changer*.

Transaction T-19 includes changing the state of the organizational artifacts that are predicted in the organizational element(s) list approved and therefore: i) changing goal(s) and sub-goal(s); ii) generate, discontinue or cancel organizational configuration element categories.

We are now able to devise the Construction Model of *organizational configuration*, represented in an Actor Transaction Diagram (Figure 3) and the corresponding Transaction Result Table.

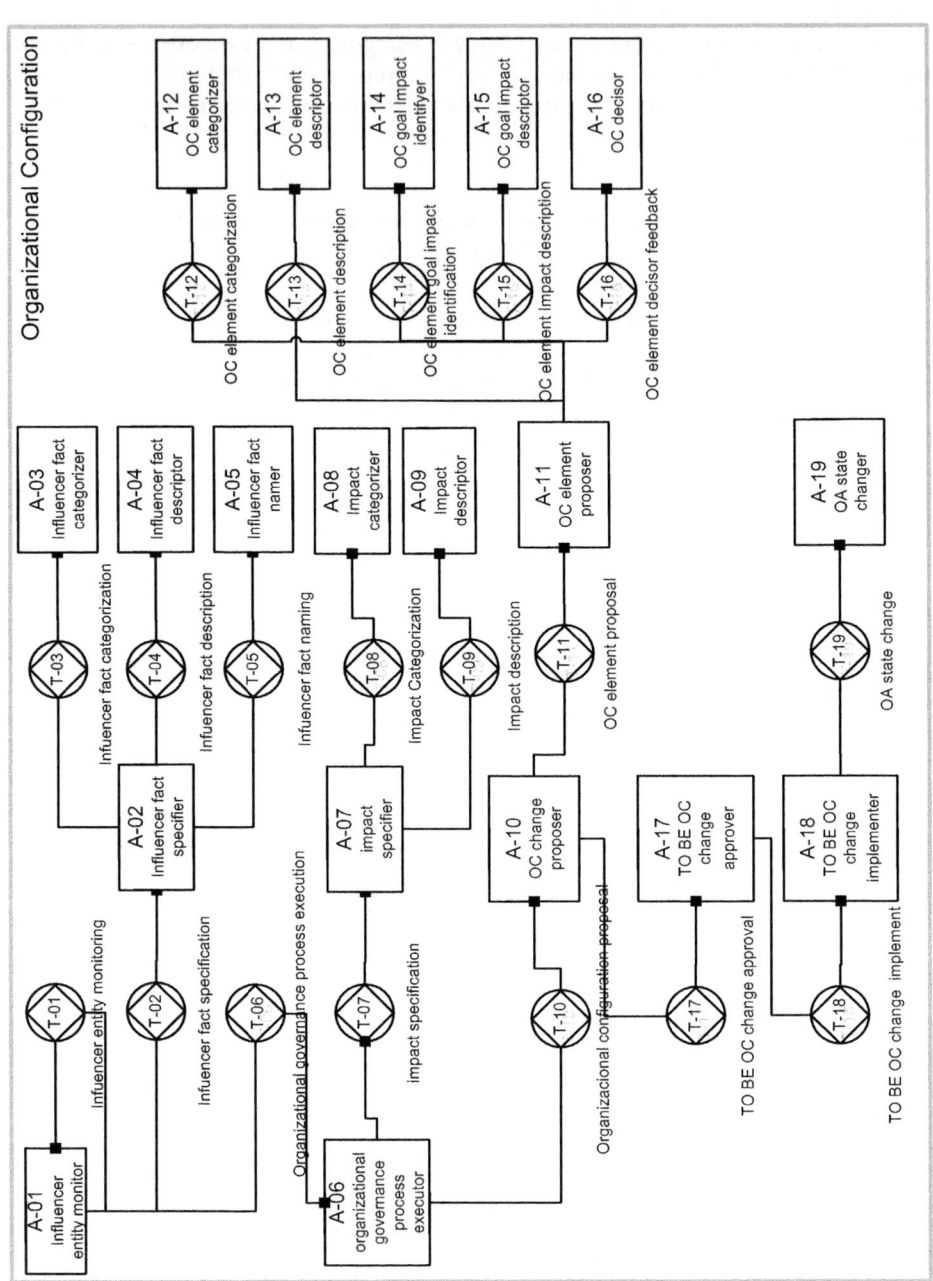

Fig. 3. Actor Transaction Diagram

Table 2 presents the resulting Transaction Result Table.

Table 2. The Transaction Result Table

Transaction Kind	Transaction Result
T01 influencer entity monitoring	R01 [influencer entity monitoring] is completed
T02 influencer fact specification	R02 [influencer fact specification] is completed
T03 influencer fact categorization	R03 [influencer fact categorization] is completed
T04 influencer fact description	R04 [influencer fact description] is completed
T05 influencer fact name	R05 [influencer fact name] is completed
T06 organizational configuration process execution	R06 [organizational configuration process execution] has started
T07 organizational configuration impact specification	R07 [organizational configuration impact specification] is completed
T08 organizational configuration impact categorization	R08 [organizational configuration impact categorization] is completed
T09 organizational configuration impact description	R09 [organizational configuration impact description] is complete
T10 organizational configuration proposal	R10 [organizational configuration proposal] is completed
T11 organizational configuration element proposal	R11 [organizational configuration element proposal] is completed
T12 organizational configuration element categorization	R12 [organizational configuration element creation categorization] is completed
T13 organizational configuration element description	R13 [organizational configuration element creation description] is completed
T14 organizational configuration element goal impact identification	R14 [organizational configuration element creation goal impact identification] is completed
T15 organizational configuration element goal impact description	R15 [organizational configuration element creation goal impact description] is completed
T16 organizational configuration element decisor feedback	R16 [organizational configuration element creation decisor feedback] is completed
T17 TO BE organizational configuration change approval	R17 [TO BE organizational configuration change approval] is completed
T18 TO BE organizational configuration plan implementation	R18 [TO BE organizational configuration plan implementation] has started
T19 OA State Change	R19 [OA State Change] has started

One note is in place for the option to consider R19 as [OA state change] has started. We assume that the time concept has to be inserted and due to time, the cancellation option has to be taken in account for the organizational artifacts that are in the process of generation/discontinuation.

5.2   Actor Role Validation

We present two examples by applying the metaphor flying the organization to an aircraft with a configuration to accomplish a mission and to an organization that provides services by using aircraft and aeronautical related resources.

Example 1

Organization O is an aircraft that has the mission to fly from point A to point E to deliver T tons of cargo at time TE. The weather alternates are points W1 and W2 and the emergency alternates are points EM1 to EM6. The aircraft transports 20 tons of cargo and has 4 crew members, member CM1 to CM4, and 4 engines. To get to point E, the organizational configuration entails a strategy of flying at flight level FL, at a cruise speed of CS and carrying T tons of fuel for an average fuel consumption of FC tons per hour (all engines). The SWOT analysis showed a potential reward in choosing that routing over others due to the unfavorable wind and a potential risk if the wind speed increases or a storm develops.

The organizational configuration presupposes that the goal is to deliver T tons of cargo (goal), at point E, at time TE (sub-goals). GOAL CATEGORY is "Mission" and DESIGN PRINCIPLES (Business rules) say that goals should be attained even if sub-goals have to be modified. The objectives are passing intermediate points B, C, and D. The means are the aircraft itself and the crew. The external influencers are the weather, specially the wind which can also be accounted for a potential risk or reward.

The aircraft takes off and climbs to the planned FL, at the planned CS, and passes W1 at the planned time. Somewhere in between B and C, crew member CM2 checks the instruments and compares the fuel count with the fuel planned and he finds out that the engines are consuming FC+2 more fuel than expected.

He registers the Influencer Fact IF at time T1 as a "Fuel consumption per hour has increased to FC+2". The IF CATEGORY is registered as "Resource malfunction" and the IF NAME is "Fuel consumption".

After being aware that the FC has increased and that can actually affect the goal, the crew initiates the process of identifying what can be done to overcome the problem and reach the goal (ORGANIZATIONAL GOVERNANCE PROCESS). To find out what needs to be done to the Organizational Configuration (ORGANIZATIONAL CONFIGURATION DESIGN PROCESS) CM3 registers the IMPACT CATEGORY as "weakness" and the IMPACT DESCRIPTION as "Problem reaching Goal due to the IF fuel consumption in excess".

A set of solutions will have to be found and, therefore, CM2 starts considering them to obtain a set of valid alternatives (ORGANIZATIONAL CONFIGURATION CHANGE PROPOSAL).

Possible solutions (OC ELEMENT) are:

– Climbing to FL+3 which would compensate for the lack of fuel and return to the hourly consumption of FC, but with an impact in time TE due to the unfavorable stronger wind speed at FL+3 (OC ELEMENT 1). CM2 registers the OC ELEMENT

CATEGORY of "Control Parameter Change", an ELEMENT DESCRIPTION of "Climbing will take less hourly fuel consumption but time to goal will be increased", an ELEMENT GOAL IMPACT IDENTIFICATION of "SUB GOAL TE will be discontinued", an ELEMENT GOAL IMPACT DESCRIPTION of "SUB GOAL TE will not be met". The DECISOR agrees that this solution is feasible.

– Dropping 5 tons of cargo would have just about the same effect with the difference that the TE will be met (OC ELEMENT 2). CM2 registers the OC ELEMENT CATEGORY of "Control Parameter Change" and an ELEMENT DESCRIPTION of "Dropping 5 tons of cargo will comply with the sub-goals however main goal will not be met", an ELEMENT GOAL IMPACT IDENTIFICATION of "GOAL will be discontinued", an ELEMENT GOAL IMPACT DESCRIPTION of "SUB GOAL will not be met". The DECISOR agrees that this solution is unfeasible under the options available.

– Landing at W1 which is closer. However since the goal is to deliver the cargo another aircraft would have to be called to deliver the cargo with an impact on time TE (OC ELEMENT 3). CM2 registers the OC ELEMENT CATEGORY of "resource bundle generator" and an ELEMENT DESCRIPTION of "Landing at W1" allows keeping current configuration, however a new aircraft has to be activated to maintain the goal although TE will not be met", an ELEMENT GOAL IMPACT IDENTIFICATION of "SUB GOALS will be discontinued", an ELEMENT GOAL IMPACT DESCRIPTION of "SUB GOALS will not be met". The DECISOR agrees that this solution is unfeasible under the options available.

CM2 builds up the ORGANIZATIONAL CONFIGURATION PROPOSAL with the details and recommends to CM1 that OC ELEMENT 1 should be taken because involves a control parameter change that will impact on a sub-goal. This new organizational configuration entails climbing immediately to FL+3, maintaining a closer look at the IF with an impact of TE+8 on sub-goal TE.

CM1 approves the proposal and the crew implements the new organizational configuration. The GOAL set is updated accordingly.

Example 2
Organization O is a company that provides air services. Among its resources are aircraft and helicopters, crew, maintenance and administrative personnel, aeronautical infrastructures (runways, towers, hangars, etc.). The company provides search and rescue alert services 24 hours per day, in 4 distinct locations and sun rise, sun set alert services in two locations. The number of yearly flying hours is FH and the yearly budget is B.

One organizational configuration goal G1 is "To have alert services in location, L5, from sun rise sun set to 24 hours a day" with 3 sub goals G1.1 "To have runway equipped with an Instrument Landing System (ILS)", G1.2 "To have housing and related facilities", G1.3 "To have night vision goggle (NVG) capability on helicopter type H and on aircraft type A". Other items included in complying with this goal are runway certification to night operation, system maintenance, system operation and training, etc. Other Goal G is to maintain the services of alert at all locations.

The company delineates its strategy to attain G1 that entails buying and certifying the system, certifying the runway for night operation, contracting and forming people to operate and maintain the ILS, G2 entails contracting civilian construction for the infrastructure building, G3 comprehends buying and installing NVG on H and A, train personnel and certify the new system.

In month M, of year Y, the company suffers a budget cut to B-10. The planning structure (PS) is informed by the financial structure that Influencer Fact IF was registered the time T1 as a "Budget cut". The IF CATEGORY is registered as "Budget" and the IF NAME is "Budget cut of B-10 has occurred".

After being aware that the available Budget has been cut to B-10 and that can actually affect goals, the planning structure initiates the process of identifying what can be done to overcome the problem (ORGANIZATIONAL GOVERNANCE PROCESS). To find out what needs to be done to the Organizational Configuration (ORGANIZATIONAL CONFIGURATION PROPOSAL) the PS registers the IMPACT CATEGORY as "weakness" and "Threat" and the IMPACT DESCRIPTION as "Problem reaching Goals due to budget cut B-10".

A set of solutions will have to be found and therefore the PS starts considering them to obtain a set of valid alternatives of B-10 containment. Possible solutions are:

- Cutting the FH in FH-4 would solve still guarantee reaching Goal G1, however Goal G would not be met (OC ELEMENT 1). The PS registers the OC ELEMENT CATEGORY of "Control Parameter Change" and an ELEMENT DESCRIPTION of "Reducing to FH-4 will allow complying to Goal G1, however, Goal G will be compromised since there's FH-4 available hours which are not enough to contain all the air activity", an ELEMENT GOAL IMPACT IDENTIFICATION of "GOAL G will be discontinued", an ELEMENT GOAL IMPACT DESCRIPTION of "GOAL G will not be met". The DECISOR agrees that this solution is unfeasible under the options available.

- Cutting G1.1 (OC ELEMENT 2). The PS registers the OC ELEMENT CATEGORY of "Resource artifact bundle generator" and an ELEMENT DESCRIPTION of "Canceling the installation and certification of ILS would compromise G1 since the H and A would not be able to perform night operations", an ELEMENT GOAL IMPACT IDENTIFICATION of "GOAL G1 will be discontinued", an ELEMENT GOAL IMPACT DESCRIPTION of "SUB GOAL G1.1 will not be met". The DECISOR agrees that this solution is unfeasible under the options available.

- Cutting G1.2 (OC ELEMENT 3). The PS registers the OC ELEMENT CATEGORY of "Resource artifact bundle generator" and an ELEMENT DESCRIPTION of "Canceling the installation and certification of ILS related infrastructure would compromise G1 since the ILS could not be operated and maintained which would cause that the H and A would not be able to perform night operations", an ELEMENT GOAL IMPACT IDENTIFICATION of "GOAL G1.2 will be discontinued", an ELEMENT GOAL IMPACT DESCRIPTION of "SUB GOAL 1.2 will not be met". The DECISOR agrees that this solution is unfeasible under the options available.

- Cutting G1.3 (OC ELEMENT 4). The PS registers the OC ELEMENT CATEGORY of "Resource artifact bundle generator" and an ELEMENT DESCRIPTION of "Canceling the installation and certification of NVG in H and A would compromise G1 since H and A would be able to perform night operations but with an elevated risk", an ELEMENT GOAL IMPACT IDENTIFICATION of "GOAL G1.3 will be discontinued", an ELEMENT GOAL IMPACT DESCRIPTION of "SUB GOAL 1.3 will not be met". The DECISOR agrees that this solution is unfeasible under the options available.

– Cutting G1.3 on A only (OC ELEMENT 5). The PS registers the OC ELEMENT CATEGORY of "Resource artifact bundle generator" and an ELEMENT DESCRIPTION of "Canceling the installation and certification of NVG in H and A would partially compromise G1.3 (A is not equipped and therefore only H would be able to perform night operations and A would be able to perform but with an elevated risk) while maintaining G1", an ELEMENT GOAL IMPACT IDENTIFICATION of "GOAL G1.3 A will be discontinued", an ELEMENT GOAL IMPACT DESCRIPTION of "SUB GOAL 1.3 A will not be met". The DECISOR agrees that this solution is feasible under the options available.

The PS builds up the ORGANIZATIONAL CONFIGURATION PROPOSAL with the details and recommends to the company chairman that OC ELEMENT 5 should be taken because involves a resource artifact bundle generator cancellation that will impact partially on a sub-goal G1.3. This new organizational configuration entails suspending the contracting of NVG to A, maintaining all other activities.

The company chairman approves the proposal and the organization implements the new organizational configuration by changing the approved OA states.

The terms *Organizational Wholeness* means that the adopted solution needs to taken into account the effect across the organization. For example, suspending contracting of NVG to A means that less hours of flight to A are needed which will impact on the number of yearly flying hours which will result in less maintenance on the support side and less training on the operational side. Since A will not maintain a 24 hours alert, less crews are needed which means that less personnel is needed and, therefore, educational and formation needs are also less. Less people involve fewer wages and reflect positively on the financial aspect.

The examples shown are deemed enough for proofing the validity and applicability of the DEMO artifact. However, we proposed to depart from an existing organizational configuration, which should always start by knowing exactly the organization's BEING and establishing the BECOMING component. This implies establishing the desired end state and setting the organizational configuration goals according to category and design principles concepts, which are comprehended in the Object Fact Diagram (not presented in this document for space reasons).

5.3   Actor Composite Roles

Section 2 proposes a set of macro composite actor roles (the performer or executor, the controller, the modeler and the decisor) that have impact on the organizational configuration. The result of applying DEMO to devising an organizational configuration shows that there are 19 actor roles.

Reverting to the original proposal we are now able to argue that these actor roles can be part of the composite actor roles with some exceptions. Depending on the organization size and on the context we identify four kinds of composite actor roles:

– The *monitor*, who is handling the arrival of influencer facts.
– The *analyst*, that assesses impact on the wholeness of the organization of a certain influencer impact and builds a proposal based on previously analyzed organizational configuration elements that entail the modification of organizational artifacts.
– The *manager*, who manages the organizational governance process.

– The *decisor*, that actually decides about the solution that will be taken to solve the influencer impact.

Use of these roles vary from organization to organization and depend heavily on the organization type, size, etc.

In a small organization, with few employees, it is normal that the owner will aggregate most of the composite actor roles identified before. In some cases, the owner will consult some of the employees that can perform analyst roles and help to devising solutions (organizational element).

In sized organizations, like the Portuguese Air Force, there are entities that perform the composite actor roles. For instance, the analyst role is performed by the several Air Staff Divisions, which build the organizational configuration elements, in a way to guarantee that the whole of the organization is affected and coordinated by the deputy commander. Once the Air Staff produces the organizational configuration change proposal, the deputy commander seeks the commander approval. The organizational artifacts included in the organizational configuration change proposal (that includes organizational configuration elements) are then implemented by the functional commands.

The previous situation is similar to most of the state organizations, characterized by pronounced hierarchical structures. This assumption will have to be subjected to further research involving those organizations.

Despite of the elaboration that was done in the previous paragraph a comparison can be made between the initial assumption of composite actor roles and the composite actor roles modeled in DEMO, presented in Figure 4.

Fig. 4. Initial composite actor roles comparison

The executor actor role runs the organizational configuration and is a valid actor role although not involved in the configuration management. The executor actor role can be of particular importance in detecting organizational configuration problems in run time and advise the controller.

The controller actor role performs an important role since he can detect problems in the running configuration or he can foresee problems depending on influencer facts that are to occur. The controller actor role can change the organizational configuration by altering some parameters. Since he is monitoring the configuration he performs the monitor actor role as well. The controller, upon detecting a problem that he cannot solve, calls the modeler to solve it. The monitor actor role performs some initial analysis and determines if the influencer fact has impact on the organizational configuration. Therefore, the controller actor role encompasses the monitor actor role although he is not constantly monitoring the external environment in order to detect relevant influencer facts. The monitor actor role performs a more preventive and pro-active actor role with a analysis capability.

The modeler actor role performs the analyst and manager actor roles since it performs the complete analysis and manages the configuration, after obtaining approval from the decisor actor role. The analyst actor role actually models the organizational configuration in a process conducted by the manager actor role. Figure 5 presents the final composite actor roles comparison.

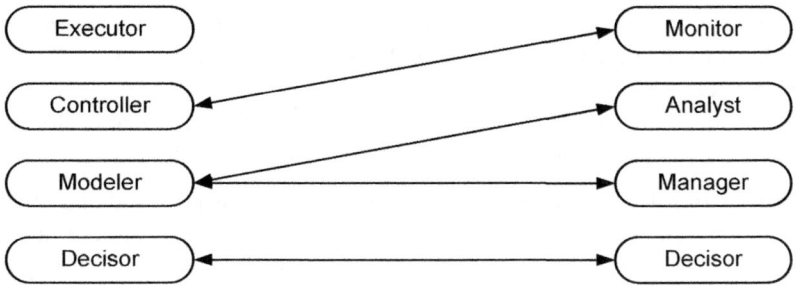

Fig. 5. Final composite actor roles comparison

6   Conclusion

Using design research methodology combined with action research methodology, we have applied the organizational configuration to the Portuguese Air Force from 2007 to 2011 (from 2007 to 2008, we have performed preparation actions such as writing business policies and business rules and from 2009 to 2011 we have conducted the transformation process).

The Portuguese Air Force is a sized organization in terms of personnel and its distribution across the structure. Therefore, composite actor roles, at the strategic level of the organization, are performed by organizational units. For instances, the analyst role is performed by the several Air Staff Divisions, which assist the Air Force Commander in the planning activities. Those planning activities result in the organizational configuration elements, enforcing that the whole of the organization is affected and coordinated by the deputy commander.

As stated before, inside the Air Force, some actor roles were impersonated, at the strategic level by the Air Staff Divisions personnel, some by institutional positions like the Air Force Commander and the Air Force Deputy Commander.

Defining an organizational configuration entails filling the organizational configuration map concepts. Performing that role requires a profound knowledge of influencer facts that can influence the desired end state. In the Air Force, the actor roles were performed as described next:

- The *monitor* actor role is performed by every department inside the Air Staff. Depending on the nature of the influencer role, each department can assess if the fact is affecting strategy and take the subject to the Air Force deputy commander to initiate the analysis change process.

- The *analyst* actor role is performed by the Air Staff departments that have specialists in several areas. These specialists come together at specific occasions, defined in the planning directives or when a specific influencer fact is detected by the *monitor*, to prepare new organizational configurations or adjust existing ones. Once the Air Staff produces the organizational configuration change proposal, the deputy commander seeks the commander approval. The organizational artifacts comprehended in the organizational configuration change proposal (that includes organizational configuration elements) are then implemented by the functional commands and inspected by the Air Force Inspection.
- The *manager*, at the strategic level is performed by the Division commanders at a first level of coordination between the Divisions and then by the Air Force deputy commander.
- The *decisor*, at the strategic level is the Air Force commander that evaluates the Air Force deputy commander proposal and approves the organizational configuration.

The organizational configuration application was implemented and the WHEN and WHO components were defined for each configuration setup, monitoring[5] and reaction mechanisms that follow the concept described in section 4. After assuming the actor roles defined in section 5, the successive changes that resulted from the economical and financial context allowed the Air Force to conduct near real time steering. Each adaptation involved revising the level of compliance, adjusting the objectives (for example, number of flying hours, number of aircraft and number of crews).

Although the explicit result numbers can not be revealed, we can state that the operational efficacy increased by over 15 % from 2007 to 2011.

As to the methodologies used, the set of seven guidelines proposed in section 3 for understanding, executing, and evaluating the research were utilized accordingly.

- **Guideline 1** – *Awareness of the Problem*. Through the organizational configuration map we propose a set of concepts, grouped on the BEING, BECOMING, BEHAVING concepts (that compose the WHAT component which is not a part of this document), which, based on the wholeness of the organization, supports organizational dimensions relation, focusing on its actors and on the dynamics between organizational dimensions when subjected to: i) multiple restrictions; ii) critical needs of real time change; iii) various configurations.
- **Guideline 2** – *Suggestion and Tentative Design of an Artifact*. In section 3, an artifact is designed for the organizational configuration and in section 5 a DEMO artifact, that supports actor role in organizational configuration change, was developed.
- **Guideline 3** – *Development*. The Tentative Design was implemented in the Portuguese Air Force. Although the work done (including a combination of technology-based artifacts, organization-based artifacts and people-based artifacts

---

[5] Three main influencer facts were under monitoring: fuel prices, budget cuts and operational and maintenance personnel leaving the Air Force.

were developed) is not described in this document, section 5 devises an artifact to represent the governance sub-organization actor role in adapting organizational configurations to influencer impact.

- **Guideline 4** – *Evaluation*. The organizational configuration design artifact and the governance sub organization actor role in changing the organizational configuration was demonstrated by using Hevner's descriptive evaluation method: *"Informed Argument – Use information from other relevant research work to build a convincing argument for the artifact's utility"* in the case of the DEMO governance sub-organization artifact and *"Scenarios – Construct detailed scenarios around the artifact to demonstrate its utility"*, in the case of the organizational configuration application. The construction and application of the Air Force Transformation was made by using the Action Research methodology. This was made by establishing objectives to be attained and by talking to people that did the work. Establishing points of contact (POC) throughout the Organization proved to be very helpful. While the work was being done, monthly reports were delivered by POC. A dashboard was also created, which proved to be very useful as it was possible to show to the decisors, almost in near real time, how the work was progressing.
- **Guideline 5** – *Conclusion and Research Contributions*. Contributions are identified in this section.
- **Guideline 6** – *Research Rigor*. The DEMO methodology provides a solid theoretical background to guarantee research rigor. The examples presented, allow verifying the artifact application and functionality.
- **Guideline 7** – *Communication of Research*. This document communicates part of the research results. Full communication is present on an unpublished thesis document untitled *Organizational and Design Engineering of the Operational and Support Dimensions of an Organization: The Portuguese Air Force Case Study* [13].

In 2009 there was the need to develop a transformation process in the Air Force [13; 25], involving the construction and implementation of a plan. Since all the Air Force was taking part of the plan, action research methodology was used to set the objectives, communicating it to people, coordinating the activities and building an organizational cockpit. Activities were performed and 24 master thesis ([26; 27] are examples) were developed (18 are already completed), each contributing to a research sub-area.

Research contributions included:

- A DEMO based design artifact that precisely and coherently specifies the following aspects of the actor role configuration perspective of an organization allowing:
  - i) continuous organization running in near real time by changing configurations since the organization map concept (WHAT) provides the basis for representing the organization extending other representations by including the link between the organization itself (BEING), where it wants to go (BECOMING) and also the instruments to control on how it is progressing (BECOMING). It also

precludes the actor roles effect on the map (WHO) and when it should be made (WHEN). Plus it relates with the G.O.D. theory extending the *microgenesis* notion to consider the whole of the organization (*macrogenesis*) in the transformation process.

- ii) better handle of expected and unexpected exceptions while keeping models continuously updated since, on one side, the organizational knowledge is maintained by constantly updating concept values in the *macrogenesis* process; on the other side, every change that is accomplished provides knowledge enrichment and allows fore planning by building different organizational configurations.

- An integrated organizational concept that allows for integrated, consistent and, in particular, efficient representation of the dynamics relationship between organizational components within several constraints. A change of organizational configuration entails a correspondent change in two dimensions: vertically due to the fact that it affects strategic objectives and, therefore, the desired results; transversally due to the fact that there's a consequent effect through out the organization as a result of an influencer impact.

- Facilitate the comprehension of the flexible organization allowing visualization of the dynamics between the operational and support components that can consider, given the complexity of processes, how to outline, organize and manage an organization, on the human and non-human resources domain, considering:

  - i) Multiple constraints as a fact of day to day influencer facts that provide a multitude of constraints. Each change has to account for the impact of all constraints in the organization's ambition in terms of objectives to be attained and act in the wholeness of the organization to allow problems that can arise of bad or untimely corrections.

  - ii) The critical needs of real time, emphasized by the need to adapt to changes rapidly maintaining the organization viability. Quick adaptation means obtaining rapidly the full impact of the influencer act on the organization's whole and providing a timely correction on the organization's path to destination, changing what is necessary, in a coherent way.

  - iii) Various configurations settings, where the need to adapt entails knowing exactly what configuration to choose or what setting to change. As the process evolves, based on the organizational knowledge bank and on the accumulated experience, a reasonable and effective organizational configuration can be developed providing less uncertainty and therefore, a clearer path.

- Facilitate the comprehension of the "traceability" of the organization's components action by determining what is the relationship between organizational concepts, in terms of the organization's processes, looking, under the soft theory, to actors participation and in what degree on the various levels of the complex organization. *Macrogenesis* actor roles can be different from organization to organization depending on culture, size and nature. However, the result of actor roles actions on the organizational configuration should be the same: react to influencer acts maintaining a viable and performative system.

- Understanding the role of governance in dealing with changes and addressing enterprise resilience, through *macrogenesis*, by configuration changing and devising the governance sub organization by applying DEMO.
- Devising the organizational configuration through the *"Macrogenesis* axiom –I Macro change"*, representing the wholeness of the organization, allowing for rapid (re)configuration of all the sub-systems in a transversal way.
- Extending [6] (re)G.O.D. work on the organizational axioms by considering and adding the wholeness of the organization by introducing the *macrogenesis* concept as follows:
  - *"Microgenesis* axiom – I change" to the *"Macrogenesis* axiom – I macro change".
  - "Organizational self-awareness axiom – I exist", extended to consider the wholeness of the organization.
  - *"Resilience* axiom – I survive", extended to consider the wholeness of the organization.
- Extending the notion of influencer and the impact of its actions on the organization.
- Devising the *macrogenesis* as the application of resilience strategies (or tactics), in a pro-active manner, to the organization wholeness in order to maintaining its viability and performance.
- Extending the concepts of "generation/discontinuation" of organizational artifacts in the G.O.D. organization to generation/discontinuation/cancellation, inserting the notion of time and allowing treating organizational artifacts that are cancelled while in the process of being generated.

We went from the *microgenesis* concept to the *macrogenesis* concept stating that any influencer act that can compromise the organization should be analyzed in the perspective of the wholeness of the organization. Using DEMO, we used the actor transaction diagram, the transaction result table and the object fact diagram to model the *macrogenesis* organization considering the effect of the WHO and the WHEN on the WHAT. We found 19 actor roles and we have aggregated those actor roles into four composite actor roles.

7   Future Work

Future research includes:

- The organizational configuration axiom and the *macrogenesis* concept should be applied to other organizations, further proven and refined on several case studies from different industry branches. It seems particularly desirable that more research be undertaken in order to continue building a set of normative artifacts to guide in practice the operation of the organizational configuration.
- Insights on how to collectively define normative outputs, the subsequent decision-making processes and which actor roles should collaborate in the production of each organizational configuration decision cycle, are essential aspects that were

addressed in this work but should be deeply addressed in future work. An analysis on how these aspects vary within different industry branches and different enterprise complexities should be considered.

– Use of DEMO should be extended to represent each organizational concept and extend its comprehension and relation. Another challenge in the scientific domain is to dive into the relations between concepts not only to formally characterize them but to also explore the unveiled potential. Concepts like organizational goal, organizational element, organizational proposal, organizational proposal approval, organizational plan implementation and organizational project (to implement) should be further delve into using DEMO to understand the small characteristics that can actually make organizational complexity a little bit more understood.

We conclude this paper by stating the importance of the composition of the WHAT (not part of this document) and the effect of the WHO and the WHEN on the organizational configuration. We validate the theory against the action research guidelines methodology and we state the contributions to the organizational scientific domain particularly on the implementation of near real time steering as: the precise definition of the business concepts that compose the organizational configuration; the *macrogenesis* concept materialized on actions taken by actor roles modeled in DEMO to adapt the organizational configuration, in its different dimensions, to influencer facts while maintaining a viable and performative state; the revealing of performance indicators that allow to ascertain the validity of the proposed theory; the reification of business concepts and the understanding of the governance in dealing with changes and addressing enterprise resilience.

References

1. Tribolet, J.: Sistemas de Informação Organizacionais. In: Amaral, L. (ed.) Organizações, Pessoas, Processos e Conhecimento: Da Reificação do Ser Humano como Componente do Conhecimento à "Consciência de Si" Organizacional, Edições Sílabo (November 2005)
2. Magalhães, R., Tribolet, J.: Engenharia Organizacional: Das Partes ao Todo e do Todo às Partes na Dialéctica entre Pessoas e Sistemas. In: Costa, S.G., Vieira, L.M., Rodrigues, J.N. (eds.) Ventos de Mudança, Fundo de Cultura. Rio de Janeiro (2009)
3. Páscoa, C., Tribolet, J.: Organizational and Design Engineering of the Operational and Support Components of an Organization: The Portuguese Air Force Case Study. In: Harmsen, F., Proper, E., Schalkwijk, F., Barjis, J., Overbeek, S. (eds.) PRET 2010. LNBIP, vol. 69, pp. 47–77. Springer, Heidelberg (2010)
4. Business Rules Group (BRG): The Business Motivation Model (2007), http://www.businessrulesgroup.org/bmm.shtml
5. Lankhorst, M.: Enterprise Architecture at Work - Modelling, Communication and Analysis. Springer, Heidelberg (2005)
6. Aveiro, D.: G.O.D. theory for organizational engineering: continuously modeling the (re)Generation, Operationalization and Discontinuation of the Enterprise, Doctoral dissertation, Department of Computer Science and Engineering, Instituto Superior Técnico, Lisboa, Portugal (2010)
7. Dietz, J.L.G.: Enterprise Ontology: Theory and Methodology. Springer, Delft (2006)
8. Dietz, J.L.G.: DEMO-3 Models and Representations (2009), http://www.demo.nl
9. Dietz, J.L.G.: DEMO-3 Way of Working (2009), http://www.demo.nl

10. Holland, J.H.: Hidden Order: How Adaptation Builds Complexity. Basic Books (1996)
11. Holland, J.H.: Emergence: From chaos to order. Oxford University Press (1998)
12. Dietz, J.L.G.: Is it $\varphi\tau\psi$ or bullshit. In: Symposium on Methodologies for Enterprise Engineering, Farewell Lecture. Delft University of Technology, Delft (2009)
13. Páscoa, C.: Organizational and Design Engineering of the Operational and Support Dimensions of an Organization: The Portuguese Air Force Case Study. Unpublished Doctoral thesis. Technical University of Lisboa, Instituto Superior Técnico, Lisboa (2012)
14. Patel, J.: 7 Simple Rules For Successful Real-Time Business Intelligence Implementation, White Paper, Business Intelligence. Dot Com. (2005)
15. Association for Information Systems (AIS): Design Research in Information Systems (2009), http://desrist.org/
    design-research-in-information-systems/ (accessed on May 19, 2010)
16. Liles, D.H., Johnson, M.E., Meade, L.: Enterprise Engineering: A discipline. In: 5th Industrial Engineering Research Conference (1996)
17. Caetano, A., Tribolet, J.: Organizational Modeling, An introduction – Part I, Department of Information Systems and Computer Science – IST, Technical University of Lisbon – Portugal (March 2007)
18. Hevner, A.R., March, S.T., Park, J., Ram, S.: Design science in information systems research. MIS Quarterly 28, 75–106 (2004)
19. Knowles, M., Moon, R.: Introducing Metaphor. Routledge, London (2006)
20. Lakoff, G., Johnson, M.: Metaphors we live by. The University of Chicago Press, Chicago (1980)
21. Morgan, G., Smircich, L.: The Case for Qualitative Research. Academy of Management Review 5(4), 491–500 (1980)
22. Brown, R.H.: A poetic for sociology. Cambridge University Press, Cambridge (1977)
23. Morgan, G.: Cybernetics and Organization Theory: Epistemology or technique? (1979) (unpublished manuscript)
24. Schon, D.: The Displacement of Concepts. Tavistock, London (1963)
25. Páscoa, C., Costa, R., Tribolet, J.: Change in the Portuguese Air Force. In: Cruz-Cunha, M.M., Varajão, J., Powell, P., Martinho, R. (eds.) CENTERIS 2011, Part I. CCIS, vol. 219, pp. 96–105. Springer, Heidelberg (2011)
26. Páscoa, C., Leal, P., Tribolet, J.: A Business Model for the Portuguese Air Force. In: Quintela Varajão, J.E., Cruz-Cunha, M.M., Putnik, G.D., Trigo, A. (eds.) CENTERIS 2010, Part II. CCIS, vol. 110, pp. 138–147. Springer, Heidelberg (2010)
27. Oliveira, T., Páscoa, C., Tribolet, J.: A Strategy Map applied to a Military Organization. In: CENTERIS 2011 Conference on ENTERprise and Information Systems, Viana do Castelo, Portugal. CCIS. Springer (October 2011)

A Method for Enterprise Architecture Alignment

Tony Clark[1], Balbir S. Barn[1], and Samia Oussena[2]

[1] Middlesex University, London, UK
[2] University of West London, UK

Abstract. Business and ICT strategic alignment remains an ongoing challenge facing organizations as they react to changing requirements by adapting or introducing new technologies to existing infrastructure. Enterprise Architecture (EA) has increasingly become relevant to these demands and as a consequence numerous methods and frameworks have emerged. However these approaches remain bloated, time-consuming and lacking in precision. This paper proposes a light-weight method for EA called LEAP and introduces a language for EA simulation that is illustrated with a detailed case study of business change currently being addressed by UK higher education institutions.

Keywords: Enterprise Architecture, Simulation, Alignment.

1 Introduction

Enterprise Architecture (EA) is intended to provide a holistic understanding of all aspects of a business, connecting the business drivers and the surrounding business environment, through the business processes, organizational units, roles and responsibilities, to the underlying IT systems that the business relies on [18]. In addition to presenting a coherent explanation of the *what, why* and *how* of a business, EA aims to support specific types of business analysis including: alignment between business functions and IT systems; business change describing the current state of a business (*as-is*) and a desired state of a business (*to-be*); maintenance of systems; checks for quality assurance and compliance; and strategic planning [9,25,20,4,13]. Alignment between business and IT strategy however remains one of the most pressing concerns [6].

EA has its origins in Zachman's original EA framework [34] but has since seen a range of methods introduced along with some specific tool modelling languages such as ArchiMate [12]. Emerging methods while purporting to address EA requirements have themselves posed questions about their efficacy. Because methods have largely been located as part of EA frameworks they do not readily provide the means by which to easily address the need to understand how to change an EA to meet a new requirement. Drilling down, the potential impact and change to an EA required would need to be promulgated as an impact analysis, a sliced view of the EA (of the systems affected), a gap analysis of missing functions and most importantly an equivalence analysis of an existing system and proposed changes. Current methods and frameworks that have largely presented layered architectural models do not necessarily lend themselves to this

E. Proper et al. (Eds.): PRET 2012, LNBIP 120, pp. 48–76, 2012.

type of modeling and analysis. Furthermore their bloated and document driven nature presents additional issues of complexity and places significant workloads on enterprise architects and those tasked with managing systems in large organization. In section 2 we discuss and review the various EA methods and frameworks currently available.

Another aspect that has potential to influence the use of an EA to address use cases such as measuring alignment between business and IT, business change or integration of new systems is the different architectural styles that may be prevalent in a single organization. Several different styles of architecture are possible. A Service Oriented Architecture (SOA) involves the publication of logically coherent groups of business functionality as interfaces, that can be used by components using synchronous or asynchronous messaging. An alternative style, argued as reducing coupling between components and thereby increasing the scope for component reuse, is Event Driven Architecture (EDA) whereby components are event generators and consumers. An important difference between SOA and EDA is that the latter generally provides scope for Complex Event Processing (CEP) where the business processes within a component are triggered by multiple, possibly temporally related, events. In SOA there is no notion of relating the invocation of a single business process to a condition holding between the data passed to a collection of calls on one of the component's interfaces. As described in [19] and [26], complex events can be the basis for a style of EA design. EDA replaces interfaces with events that trigger organizational activities. This creates the flexibility necessary to adapt to changing circumstances and makes it possible to generate new processes by a sequence of events [22]. The relationship between event driven SOA and EA is described in [2] where a framework is proposed that allows enterprise architects to formulate and analyze research questions including 'how to model and plan EA-evolution to SOA-style in a holistic way' and 'how to model the enterprise on a formal basis so that further research for automation can be done.' Our claim is that system architectures should be based on both EDA and SOA.

Technologies for EA need to support a wide spectrum of business concepts and use-cases. When designing such technologies there are essentially two approaches: top-down or *analytic* and bottom-up or *synthetic*. The former characteristically identifies all potentially distinct categories of feature from the domain with the goal of equipping the user with a richly diverse collection of elements with which to express their models. The approach guarantees to provide a sufficiently expressive language at the expense of precision and orthogonality. The latter characteristically identifies a precisely defined collection of orthogonal concepts with associated semantics; the goal is to achieve precision with respect to a collection of defined use-cases, as opposed to the the more holistic, but imprecise, top-down approach.

There is safety in the analytic approach, it is guaranteed to be complete mostly because of its ambiguity and rich collection of features. However this safety is misleading since the resulting language is not amenable to mechanical processing and rigorous analysis. Therefore, top-down languages are forever consigned to the early stages of system analysis and design where so-called *sketching* is an important modelling technique.

So how dangerous is the synthetic approach? Certainly it is almost guaranteed to be incomplete since the design of the language must be contextualized with particular use-cases. However, this might lead to a language that is *good enough* for most cases, and as such will have engineering benefits that far outweigh those of a sketching language. In addition, a synthetic language provides a firm basis for iterative language development through the incremental analysis of new use-cases.

EA languages are currently exclusively top-down. They are large and imprecise and therefore almost guaranteed to support any interpretation of a business and associated EA use-case. Typically, an EA language makes distinctions between different views of a business, for example separating business, application and technology layers. The result is a very large number of suspiciously similar features. Our proposal is that this is not necessary, and that the multiplicity of feature variety and separation of views is bogus, at least fundamentally[1].

This paper validates the claim that EA technologies should be synthetic by introducing and using a technology called LEAP to analyse a problem faced by UK universities. The case study involves the specification of an idealized system that meets a new organizational regulation, then shows how the current IT systems can be used to implement the system and finally describes a process by which the two architectures can be aligned. It is precisely because LEAP is a synthetic operational language for architecture simulation that the user can have confidence in the alignment, in contrast to other enterprise modelling technologies. The approach has been used to describe concrete IT systems within our own organization and to indicate appropriate modifications necessary to meet new regulations. Our contribution claim is that LEAP represents a novel approach to EA in that it is a simple, precise and executable technology that offers a different approach to EA analysis with the advantages that come with the ability to analyze and simulate an architecture.

2   Related Work on EA Methods

The nature of EA, that is, its breadth, the range of organizational impact and the inherent complexity of operating at multiple levels (business through to deployment) and technology variations means that it is difficult to arrive at specific understanding of what methodologies are available and the extent of their utilization. As Riege et al point out: '*Although there are isolated EA methods taking the situation of application into account,..., there is no overall landscape of EA methods available*' [25, :p389]. In addition, the practitioner nature of EA also means that well documented methods are difficult to access. In order to establish the current availability and literature surrounding EA methods, key word searches '*Enterprise Architecture Method*' were conducted in Google Scholar and the ACM/IEEE digital libraries. This section presents an overview

---

[1] How it is presented to a business user is entirely a different matter.

of the current situation and while it is not an exhaustive literature review (the limitations of the paper and its main focus prevents that) it does allow the reader an insight into the state of the art.

Much literature has concentrated on providing descriptions of a number of architecture frameworks. Usefully Steen et al point out: '*Frameworks provide structure to the architectural descriptions by identifying and sometimes relating different architectural domains and the modelling techniques associated with them*' [28, :p6]. Some of the more popular and widely disseminated EA frameworks include:

Zachman's Framework that provides a logical structure for classifying and organizing representations of an EA relevant to specific stakeholders in terms of 36 different types of views [34];

The Reference Model for Open Distributed Processing (RM-ODP) is an ISO/ITU Standard (ITU, 1996) that defines a framework for architecture specification of large distributed systems using five viewpoints on a system and its environment: enterprise, information, computation, engineering and technology. The theoretical basis of the RM-ODP model resides in object oriented principles and service oriented specification and the mapping of the levels to implementation objects [15,24];

The Open Group's framework TOGAF [27] and related frameworks for the Department of Defense (DODAF [33]), Federal processing (FEAF), UK Ministry of Defence (MODAF) [3] provides over-arching structures for supporting a consistent approach for standardizing, planning, analyzing and modelling of architectural system components.

Regardless of the specifics of the framework, as Tang et al note there are common deficiencies such as: (1) the level of detail required in an architecture model is not generally specified; (2) support, specification and management of non-functional requirements is lacking and (3) software configuration modelling is also generally lacking [29]. Although architecture includes notions of design, the objective of architecture is different from design but there are a lack of guidelines to address the case when architectural activity moves into detailed design.

The frameworks discussed above claim independence of any specific method. In addition to the availability of these frameworks, a number of methods aimed at delivering techniques, languages and tools to support EA have also been developed. The ADM method underpinning TOGAF is one exception. Methods have focused on specific aspects of business and IT alignment [30,31] (an oft cited requirement [6]) or they have provided a means of providing analysis tools for understanding EA changes and impact [17,16]. Of note also is the UN/CE-FACT modelling method - a UML based approach to design business services that are focused on collaboration with external organizations [14]. Like [11]this method introduces the notion of the extended enterprise architecture that includes external system components (located in other organizations) that require collaboration.

There are examples of methods that have a more generic EA purpose. These methods do not focus on typical use cases for EA, instead they are aimed at addressing the design gap introduced earlier and identified by [29]. An early example is Memo [10] an EA method that introduces a range of visual modelling languages supporting multiple views. The method provides an integrated process model. Some of the approaches proposed could be argued to have been superseded by advances in business process modelling notably with the advent of BPMN (Business Process Modelling Notation) and service oriented architectures. Pereira and Sousa [23] introduce a method that is overlayed on top of the Zachman framework and suggests how specific techniques can be used to develop each of the 36 viewpoints. Integration of artifacts produced for the viewpoints is also suggested. Support for Event modelling is not immediately clear in this method. The SOMA method developed by Arsanjani et al for IBM is an end-end software development life-cycle method that assumes a service oriented architecture style for EA. The method uses concepts of component based design and goal oriented modelling as well as established techniques such as use case modelling to support the design and implementation of EA solutions [1]. While the language and concepts underpinning SOMA have some similarity with the method and technology proposed in this paper, we note that consistent with all the methods reviewed here, there is not immediate clarity on how event modelling is integrated and supported in these methods.

The range and variation of methods in terms of focus and scope strongly supports the case proposed by Riege et al that there is no method that fits all the requirements for EA and instead there is a need for a method engineering approach [25]. They identify three broad contingency factors that should influence the target focus for EA methods: Adoption of advanced architectural paradigms and modelling capabilities; Deployment and monitoring of EA data and services and Organizational penetration of EA. We argue that that methods also need to ensure that they address the key use cases for EA such as business and IT alignment.

Our claim is that many EA use-cases can be addressed using a precisely defined synthetic language compared to the imprecise analytic technologies currently available. To validate this claim we have constructed a technology called LEAP that is briefly introduced in section 3 where it is compared with a leading EA technology. We have applied LEAP to a number of real-world case studies such as that described in section 6, however because these become rather large, section 4 describes a complete LEAP application using a simple example. We do not claim that LEAP will support *every* EA use-case, however our aim to address a series of use-cases and incrementally extend LEAP. This paper argues that LEAP represents a practical technology for Architecture Alignment and our approach is defined in section 5.

3   LEAP

The LEAP language proposes that EA is fundamentally about representing and analyzing data-rich and highly-structured executable systems at different levels of abstraction. It has been designed as a synthetic language where distinctions between many business concepts are deemed fundamentally irrelevant (domain specific presentation issues being viewed as perfectly respectable sugar). The key concepts in LEAP are:

component. A component is the key structuring concept in LEAP and can be used to represent entities such as physical systems, roles, logical systems, transient elements, and organizational units. Components encapsulate data, behaviour, conditions such as business directives and goals, and can be nested. Components are intended to support a process of step-wise refinement where a business can be expressed as a single component at a high-level of abstraction and where refinement develops a graph of sub-components.

data. Each component defines models of data; shared models support information communication between components. Data is highly structured, including lists and records, to facilitate declarative pattern matching.

functions. LEAP is a functional language. Functions can be attached to components to represent business processes and can be used at any level to parameterize over language features. For example, parameterizing over components supports template patterns.

messages. LEAP execution is performed in terms of messages between component ports. Messages are defined in port interfaces and bear model data. Execution strategies for both SOA and EDA are supported through the construction and use of component architectures based on the same fundamental concepts.

rules. Component behaviour can be specified in terms of rules that match against data in the local database and messages arriving at the component's ports. Rules facilitate complex event processing since a rule may rely on receiving multiple unordered interrelated messages and database changes of arbitrary complexity. Where appropriate, rule collections can be expressed using state machines within components.

conditions. Business goals and directives can be expressed using invariants over the state of a component and its sub-components. Component behaviour can be expressed in terms of pre and post-conditions.

LEAP has a precise semantics in the form of an operational implementation and an associated tool for graphical display and simulation. Our claim is that the features above are necessary and sufficient for a wide range of EA use-cases, and there they are not sufficient, a conservative extension will suffice.

Table 1 shows a comparison between ArchiMate concepts and LEAP concepts. We have chosen ArchiMate because it is arguably the most developed EA notation. The table shows that ArchiMate includes a large number of different elements that can be mapped onto a smaller number of LEAP elements. In fact, ArchiMate includes more elements that those shown because several of the concepts occur as distinct elements in different layers. Our claim is that this mapping provides evidence that EA languages, and ArchiMate in particular,

Table 1. Comparison of Archimate and LEAP

Archimate Concept	LEAP Concept
Actor	Component
Application Layer	Components
Artifact	Data Model
Behaviour	Operation,rule, transition
Business Function	Operation, rule, transition
Business Layer	Components
Business Process	Operation, rule, transition
Business Service	Operation, rule, transition
Collaboration	Components
Collective Behaviour	Components
Communication Path	Connections
Concept	Component,Class
Contract	Invariant
Device	Component
External Perspective	LEAP Model
Individual Behaviour	Component
Interaction	Mesage
Interface	Interface
Internal Perspective	LEAP Model
Meaning	Semantics
Network	Component
Product	Data Model
Representation	Data Model
Role	Component
Software	Component
Technology Layer	Components
Value	?

includes redundancy that is difficult to analyze without mapping to a language with precise semantics.

It should be stated that LEAP does not claim to be an Architecture Description Language, although it shares many features with technologies for ADL. Features of LEAP can be used to model both physical and logical aspects of a system including information, roles and organizational units. Furthermore, although LEAP has an operational semantics, there is no support for expressing complex features such as real-time.

LEAP is a text-based language together with a graphical modelling tool. Figure 1 shows the core language features. A LEAP model consists of a collection of a collection of nested component definitions. A component has input and output ports from which it reads and to which it writes messages. Ports are typed with interfaces. Each component manages a database whose tables are defined as classes and associations in a data model. the database can be initialized using a **state** declaration and a component is initialized by the **init** expressions that are evaluated when the component is created. Incoming messages are handled by operations. An operation may update the component's database by adding and removing data; changes in the database are monitored by a collection of rules. When a rules patterns all match the current state of the database, the body of the rule is performed.

```
exp ::=
  cmp
| fun(arg*) exp          functions
| exp(exp*)              applications
| var                    variables
| atom                   ints,strs,bools
| state                  local data
| self                   reference
| { exp* }               blocks
| { bind* }              records
| [ exp | qual* ]        lists
| new term               extension
| term                   terms
| delete term            deletion
| if exp then exp else exp   conditional
| replace pattern with term else exp
| find pattern in exp exp else exp
| case exp { arm* }      matching
| let bind* in exp       locals
| for pattern in exp { exp } loops
| forall pattern in exp { exp } univ quant
| exp <- name(exp*)      message passing
term  ::= name(exp*)
arm   ::= pattern -> exp
bind  ::= pattern = exp
qual  ::= pattern <- exp | ?exp
```

```
cmp ::=                          components
  component [name] {             optional name
    port*                        input/output ports
    [model { element* }]         data models
    [state { term* }]            local data
    [invariants { inv* }]        always hold
    [operations { op* }]         methods
    [rules { rule* }]            event processing
    [init { exp* }               initialization
    (name = exp)*                bindings
  }
port ::=
  port name[(in|out)]: interface { message }
element ::=
  class name { (name:type)* }
| assoc name { name type name type }
pattern ::=
  var                            variables
| name(pattern*)                 term patterns
| atom                           ints,strs,bools
| name = pattern                 pattern binding
| [pattern*]                     lists
| pattern:pattern                cons pairs
| ? exp                          predicate
op    ::= name(arg*) { exp* }
rule  ::= name : pattern* { exp* }
```

Fig. 1. LEAP Language

4   A Simple LEAP Example

The people of Ruritania adore fruit, especially apples and oranges. However, an increase in the voracious Ruritanian Fruiter Beetle (*Greengrocerous Apostrophorum*) means that availability must be limited so that each Ruritanian can have either apples or oranges, but not both, each day. Typically a Ruritanian fruit shop will sell apples and oranges at separate tills, merging the account at the end of each day. However this makes it difficult to police the fruit quotas. A new system must be implemented that enforces the rules until the beetle can be eradicated.

Our business goal in this case is to enforce the regulations. Our approach is to design an idealized architecture that satisfies the regulation and then to extend the current fruit shop architecture in such a way that it is possible to show how the physical architecture is consistent with the logical architecture. Our claim is that this EA use-case is supported by LEAP because it has a precisely defined behaviour.

4.1   Logical Architecture

The first step in EA Alignment is to define the logical architecture. Typically this will create a single component definition that captures the logical information and behaviour together with any constraints that must be achieved. Figure 2

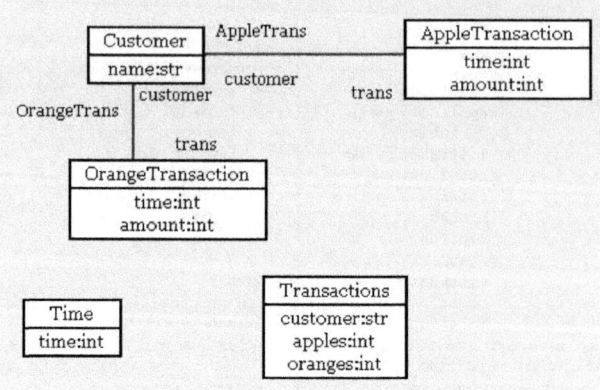

Fig. 2. Greengrocer Information

shows the information managed by each Ruritanian greengrocer. The business goal is specified as the following LEAP invariant:

```
illegal_to_buy_both_products_on_same_day {
  exists OrangeTrans(c,OrangeTransaction(t,_)) in state {
    exists AppleTrans(c,AppleTransaction(t,_)) in state { false }
  }
}
```

Simulation of the logical component is achieved by defining a LEAP component that sends messages to a greengrocers shop component as shown in figure 3. The definition of component `logical_architecture_simulation` includes the definition of the logical architecture named `greengrocers`. The simulation component has a predefined state that contains a sequence of messages each of which has a time, a message name and a sequence of arguments. There are two simulation rules: `send` that fires when there is a message at the current time, and `tick` that fires when there is no message at the current time and when the end of the simulation has not been reached. The `send` rule sends the message to the input port of the greengrocer component. The `tick` rule increments the time and sends a `tick` message to the greengrocer. The logical component is defined in figure 4. The port named `in` can receive messages named `buy_apples`, `buy_oranges` and `tick`. Each message is handled by an operation with the same name. Consider `buy_apples`, it uses the private local operation `get_customer` to select a term from the component's database (named `state`) if it exists or create a new customer-term if it does not. The `buy_apples` operation proceeds by querying the database for the current time and then adding two new database terms that represent an apple transaction.

The `greengrocer` component has a rule named `day` that is run once per day in order to consolidate the accounts. Rules are checked each time a message arrives or when the database changes in a component. In this case all the transactions for the customer in the given day are added up and a new consolidated `Transactions` term is added to the database.

```
component logical_architecture_simulation {
  component greengrocers {
    // Defined elsewhere...
  }
  state {
    Time(0)
    Message(0,'buy_oranges',['fred',10])
    Message(1,'buy_apples',['fred',10])
    Message(2,'buy_oranges',['fred',10])
    Message(3,'buy_apples',['fred',10])
    Message(4,'buy_oranges',['fred',10])
    Message(4,'buy_apples',['fred',10])
    End(5)
  }
  rules {
    send: Time(t) Message(t,m,args) {
      send(greengrocers.in,m,args);
      delete Message(t,m,args)
    }
    tick: Time(t) not(Message(t,_,_)) not(End(t)) {
      delete Time(t);
      greengrocers.in <- tick();
      new Time(t+1)
    }
  }
}
```

Fig. 3. Simulation Component

```
component greengrocers {
  model { // As shown in figure Greengrocer Information ... }
  invariants { // The illegal_to_buy_both_products_on_same_day condition... }
  port in[in]: interface {
    buy_apples(name:str,amount:int):void;
    buy_oranges(name:str,amount:int):void;
    tick():void
  }
  operations {
    buy_apples(customer,amount) {
      let c = get_customer(customer); t = time()
      in new AppleTransaction(t,amount), AppleTrans(c,AppleTransaction(t,amount))
    }
    buy_oranges(customer,amount) { // As above for oranges... }
    get_customer(name) { find Customer(name) in state else new Customer(name) }
    time() { find Time(t) in state { t } else 0 }
    tick() { replace Time(t) with Time(t+1) else new Time(1) }
    addup(l) { case l { [] -> 0; h:t -> h + addup(t) } }
  }
  rules {
    day: Time(t) {
      for Customer(name) in state {
        let oranges = addup([n | OrangeTrans(Customer(name),OrangeTransaction(tt,n)) <- state, ?(tt <= t) ]);
            apples = addup([n | AppleTrans(Customer(name),AppleTransaction(tt,n)) <- state, ?(tt <= t) ])
        in replace Transactions(name,a,o) with Transactions(name,apples,oranges)
          else new Transactions(name,apples,oranges)
      }
    }
  }
}
```

Fig. 4. The Logical Greengrocers Component

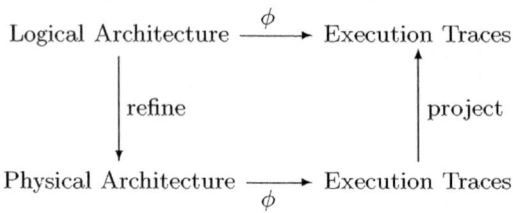

Fig. 5. Architecture Refinement

4.2   Refinement

LEAP has an executable semantics which means that a LEAP model can be mapped to execution traces. Figure 5 is an overview of the approach for architecture alignment. A Logical Architecture, such as that described for Ruritanian **greengrocers** is mapped to execution traces via a semantic function ϕ. A Physical Architecture is constructed using the real-world systems available to the organization leading to a collection of physical execution traces. It remains to show that the physical architecture is *complete* and *consistent*. Completeness is achieved by showing that there is a physical trace for every correct logical trace and consistency is achieved by showing that every physical trace can be projected onto a correct logical trace, subject to preserving key information.

Table 2. Logical Architecture Execution Trace

component	in	state
greengrocers	buy_oranges('fred',10)	
greengrocers	tick()	OrangeTrans(Customer('fred'), OrangeTransaction(0,10)), OrangeTransaction(0,10), Customer('fred')
greengrocers	buy_apples('fred',10)	Transactions('fred',0,10), Time(1),...
greengrocers	tick()	AppleTrans(Customer('fred'), AppleTransaction(1,10)), AppleTransaction(1,10),...
greengrocers	buy_oranges('fred',10)	Transactions('fred',10,10), Time(2),...
greengrocers	tick()	OrangeTrans(Customer('fred'), OrangeTransaction(2,10)), OrangeTransaction(2,10), Transactions('fred',10,10), Time(2), ...
greengrocers	buy_apples('fred',10)	Transactions('fred',10,20), Time(3),...
greengrocers	tick()	AppleTrans(Customer('fred'), AppleTransaction(3,10)), AppleTransaction(3,10), Transactions('fred',10,20), Time(3), ...
greengrocers	buy_apples('fred',10)	Transactions('fred',20,20), Time(4), ...
greengrocers	buy_oranges('fred',10)	AppleTrans(Customer('fred'), AppleTransaction(4,10)), AppleTransaction(4,10), Transactions('fred',20,20), Time(4), ...
greengrocers	tick()	OrangeTrans(Customer('fred'), OrangeTransaction(4,10)), OrangeTransaction(4,10), ...
greengrocers		Transactions('fred',30,30), Time(5), ...

Given that LEAP has a precisely defined semantics (currently implemented as a tool for executing LEAP models), it would be possible to formally establish the refinement criteria. In practice however, it is likely that rigorous inspection of traces will be sufficient to provide confidence of correct refinement. The LEAP tool can produce an XML trace of a model execution. The table shown in table 2 is a symbolic representation of the output for the greengrocer simulation where execution proceeds from top to bottom and repeated state is represented by ellipses.

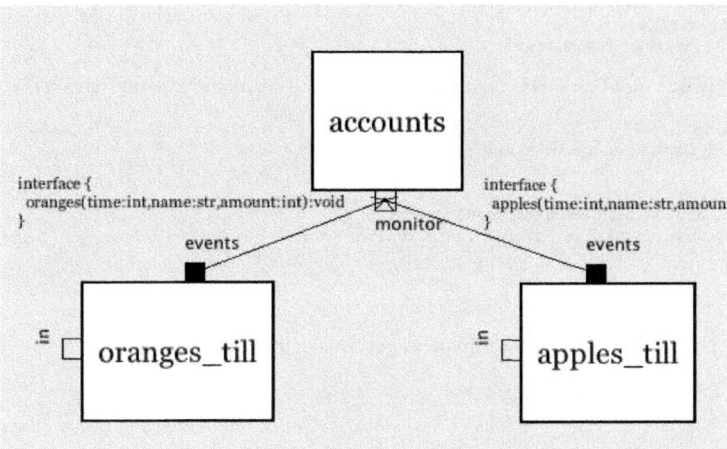

Fig. 6. Ruriatian Greengrocers: Physical Architecture

4.3   Physical Architecture

A physical architecture must reflect the systems available to an organization. All Ruritanian Greengrocers must, by law, implement separate tills for apples and oranges. Therefore, they have separate IT systems that must be consolidated in order to implement the new regulations. The consolidation is achieved by a new IT system, called accounts, as shown in figure 6. Notice that the two tills have output ports that produce events; a third party component can monitor the events in order to detect changes. The simulation component must be modified slightly to reflect the physical architecture as shown in figure 7. The two till components are almost identical, therefore they are candidates for *template patterns*. LEAP can represent template patterns by abstracting a function over a component definition. Each till behaves exactly the same except for the type of produce being sold, therefore the physical architecture simulator defines the make_till operation defined in figure 8. Now it is possible to create both types of till using the function:

```
component physical_architecture_simulation {
  state {
    Time(0)
    Message(0,oranges_till.in,'buy',['fred',10])
    Message(1,apples_till.in,'buy',['fred',10])
    Message(2,oranges_till.in,'buy',['fred',10])
    Message(3,apples_till.in,'buy',['fred',10])
    Message(4,apples_till.in,'buy',['fred',10])
    Message(4,oranges_till.in,'buy',['fred',10])
    End(5)
  }
  rules {
    send: Time(t) Message(t,p,m,args) {
      send(p,m,args);
      delete Message(t,p,m,args)
    }
    tick: Time(t) not(Message(t,_,_,_)) not(End(t)) { replace Time(t) with Time(t+1) }
  }
  operations {
    time() { find Time(t) in state else 0 }
  }
  init {
    connect(apples_till.events,accounts.monitor);
    connect(oranges_till.events,accounts.monitor)
  }
}
```

Fig. 7. Physical Architecture Simulation

```
make_till(type) {
  component {
    model {
      class Customer { name:str }
      class Transaction { type:str; time:int; amount:int }
      assoc Trans { customer Customer trans Transaction }
    }
    port in[in]: interface {
      buy(name:str,amount:int):void
    }
    port events[out]: interface {
      buy(type:str,time:int,name:str,amount:int):void
    }
    operations {
      buy(customer,amount) {
        let c = get_customer(customer)
        in {
          new Transaction(type,time(),amount);
          new Trans(c,Transaction(type,time(),amount));
          events <- buy(type,time(),customer,amount)
        }
      }
      get_customer(name) {
        find Customer(name) in state else new Customer(name)
      }
    }
  }
}
```

Fig. 8. The make_till Operation

```
component physical_architecture_simulation {
  operations {
    make_till(type) { ... }
  }
  oranges_till = make_till('oranges')
  apples_till = make_till('apples')
  ...
}
```

The accounts component monitors the events created by the till components, must consolidate the accounts and must detect fraud when it occurs. The physical definition of the new system is shown in figure 9. The execution trace for the physical architecture is shown in table 3. At the end of the trace, the system reports fraud because the customer has attempted to buy apples and oranges on the same day.

It remains to show that the physical architecture is correct with respect to the logical architecture. In an ideal world we would formally prove this to be the case. However, in a practical setting, where architectures may be large and where expertise with formal methods is limited, we argue that is more realistic to be able to use rigorous argument through inspection, to provide confidence of correctness. Since LEAP provides modular components, operational semantics and execution traces, it is possible to generate execution data that can be inspected off-line.

```
component accounts {
  model {
    class Transactions { customer:str; apples:int; oranges:int }
  }
  port monitor[in]: interface {
    buy(type:str,time:int,customer:str,amount:int):void
  }
  operations {
    buy(type,t,customer,amount) {
      case type {
        'apples' -> new Apples(t,customer,amount);
        'oranges' -> new Oranges(t,customer,amount)
      }
    }
  }
  rules {
    record_apples: Apples(t,customer,amount) not(Oranges(t,customer,_)) {
      replace Transactions(customer,apples_bought,oranges_bought) with
        Transactions(customer,apples_bought+amount,oranges_bought)
      else new Transactions(customer,amount,0)
    }
    record_oranges: Oranges(t,customer,amount) not(Apples(t,customer,_)) {
      replace Transactions(customer,apples_bought,oranges_bought) with
        Transactions(customer,apples_bought,oranges_bought+amount)
      else new Transactions(customer,0,amount)
    }
    fraud: Oranges(t,customer,_) Apples(t,customer,_) {
      print('FRAUD: ' + customer + ' at time ' + t + ' ' + state)
    }
  }
}
```

Fig. 9. Physical Definition for accounts

In the case of the Ruritanian Greengrocers system, we need to show that execution traces such as those shown above satisfy correctness. Consider transforming the physical trace into the logical trace. The two till components can be transformed into their logical counterpart by re-introducing type information. The accounts component is almost equivalent to the information held in the logical component and can be trivially transformed. Messages that purchase apples and oranges can be transformed by reintroducing type information, and `tick` messages can be introduced when the time changes. Therefore, we argue that the physical trace is consistent with the logical trace.

It remains to show that every correct logical execution has an equivalent physical execution. To see this we argue as follows. Every `buy_oranges` and `buy_apples` message is translated to a `buy` message that targets the appropriate till component. The effect of these messages on the tills and accounts has the desired effect. The `tick` messages are removed, but they occur when no other messages are being processed and have the same effect in the physical architecture.

5   An Approach to Architecture Alignment

In this section we introduce our approach to using LEAP for Architecture Alignment. The motivation for developing a method to support EA is driven by our hypothesis that existing methods are large, cumbersome, and are not based on precisely defined concepts. Where methods have used modeling languages such as ArchiMate they are constrained by orthodox layering approaches (business layer, functional layer, deployment layer and so on) that prevent rigorous equivalence analysis. Our proposed method also uses existing techniques to identify key information, but then represents it using a precisely defined simulation language. Figure 10 provides an overview of our proposed method.

Consistent with most approaches to EA methods where there is need to describe *as-is* and *to-be* models, there are two streams of activity which converge at key stages. The *to-be* analysis stream includes activities to **Model Requirements**. We do not prescribe how you might wish to derive the requirements in order to produce a model of requirements but as our method is based on UML-style modelling, models will include artifacts such as business information models, process models and business use case models. Existing method approaches such as Catalysis [8] and its derivatives [7] could be used for developing information models whilst recommended approaches for process modeling could include Ould's approach [21].

In parallel to the **Model Requirements** step, the activities in the **Collate Physical Architecture** stage will bring together existing descriptions of systems and their configurations. Our experience of such descriptions are large pictorial based documentation captured using drawing tools such as Powerpoint. A key output of this stage is a description of the systems that exist in the organization. We recommend capturing the description of each system as a UML Component to aid the migration to later stages of the method. Again, the method

Table 3. Physical Architecture Execution Trace

id	in	state
oranges_till	buy('fred',10)	
oranges_till		Trans(Customer('fred'), Transaction('oranges',0,10)), Transaction('oranges',0,10), Customer('fred')
accounts	buy('oranges',0,'fred',10)	
apples_till	buy('fred',10)	
accounts		Transactions('fred',0,10), Oranges(0,'fred',10)
apples_till		Trans(Customer('fred'), Transaction('apples',1,10)), Transaction('apples',1,10), Customer('fred')
accounts	buy('apples',1,'fred',10)	...
oranges_till	buy('fred',10)	...
accounts		Transactions('fred',10,10), Apples(1,'fred',10), Oranges(0,'fred',10)
oranges_till		Trans(Customer('fred'),Transaction('oranges',2,10)), Transaction('oranges',2,10), ...
accounts	buy('oranges',2,'fred',10)	...
apples_till	buy('oranges',2,'fred',10)	...
accounts		Transactions('fred',10,20), Oranges(2,'fred',10), Apples(1,'fred',10), Oranges(0,'fred',10)
apples_till		Trans(Customer('fred'),Transaction('apples',3,10)), Transaction('apples',3,10), ...
accounts	buy('apples',3,'fred',10)	...
accounts		Transactions('fred',20,20), Apples(3,'fred',10), Oranges(2,'fred',10), Apples(1,'fred',10), Oranges(0,'fred',10)
oranges_till		Trans(Customer('fred'),Transaction('oranges',4,10)), Transaction('oranges',4,10), ...
apples_till	buy('fred',10)	...
accounts	buy('oranges',4,'fred',10)	...
apples_till		Trans(Customer('fred'),Transaction('apples',4,10)), Transaction('apples',4,10),...
accounts	buy('apples',4,'fred',10)	Transactions('fred',20,30),...

does not prescribe new approaches, it leaves it to the practitioner to determine how to produce the artifacts required.

The **Configure Physical Architecture** step slices a description of an EA to determine what system components are likely to be impacted by emerging requirements. Techniques that can be used to support this impact analysis includes use case maps [5]. A use case map is simply a trace of path of causal sequences of events across a set of system components representing an EA. The events are triggered by a business use case identified in the **Model Requirements** step.

Alternative approaches that could be used in this step include the use of CRC to help identify those system components that are (collaboratively) responsible for delivering a business use case [32]. The key output from this activity is an artifact expressed in system components that includes all the EA system elements that will be subject to some impact as a result of the emerging requirements.

Up to now, the steps in the method have utilized well-established notations and techniques. The subsequent steps in stage 2 incorporate an integrated set of concepts from SOA and complex event processing.

The **Define Physical Enterprise Architecture (L-EA)** step is aimed at defining a slice of the existing physical architecture that we know will be subject to impact from new requirements. The slice emerged from the **Configure**

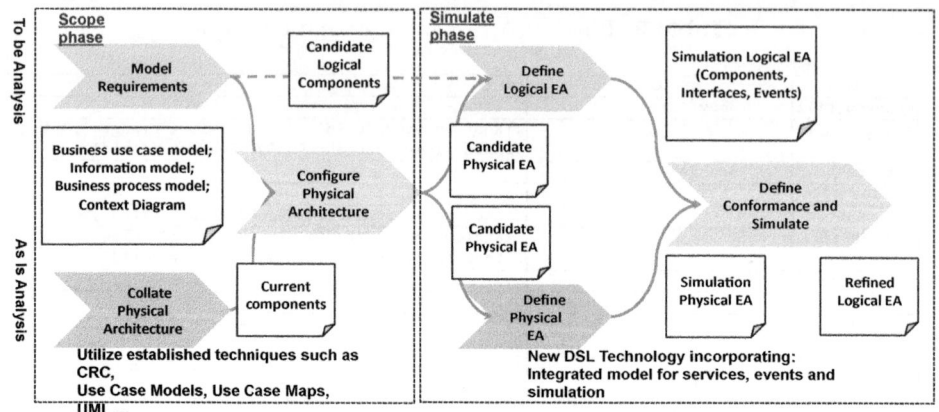

Fig. 10. Method Overview

Physical Architecture step and like the Logical EA step is now expressed in our DSL using concepts such as components, ports, rules and events.

The **Define Logical Enterprise Architecture (L-EA)** step produces a model based description of a target logical EA - that is - the system components, information structures and constraints that are required as a result of the Model Requirements step. Where appropriate the Logical EA may use candidate logical components from the Configure Physical Architecture step.

The Logical EA (L-EA) uses our integrated concepts derived from SOA and complex event modeling so the L-EA is expressed as components offering services, raised events, requested services and monitored events. Dependencies between components are thus expressed in terms of services request and fulfillments and event management.

The **Conformance** step uses simulation to produce and visualize results. The logical architecture describes what is required and the physical *to-be* architecture defines how existing systems can be used to satisfy the requirements. It remains to validate the physical architecture by showing that the behavior conforms to the requirements. If the simulation produces the same output when it is run with both the logical and physical EA definitions then we claim that they are *aligned*. Such an approach presents a practical solution that is geared toward EA practitioners.

6   Case Study

Having outlined the method and technology, this section presents a genuine requirement faced by IT directors in UK higher education institutions to deliver key information sets (KIS) to applicants deciding on which course and which university to chose for study at undergraduate level.

Higher education institutions (HEI) in the UK are faced with a challenging and dynamic business environment where public funding of HEIs has been reduced by up to 70%. This lost funding is being replaced by the introduction of a new student fees regime beginning in 2012 following a bill introduced in the UK Parliament in November 2010. The UK Government is of the view that students will require key information in order to make informed decisions regarding the selection of courses and institutions. Currently this information is not readily available in a consistent and easily accessible form. Consequently the Higher Education funding body (HEFCE) is coordinating the specification of the required information and how it is to be made available and at what time.

HEFCE produces KIS data at a given census date each year. In order to be included in KIS, each university must register with both the NSS and DHLE government agencies before the census date. KIS information consists of NSS data, teaching and learning data from each university, financial data from each university (including university owned and private accommodation costs), employability data from the DHLE agency.

The NSS data is completed by students via a web portal. The details of the information go to the NSS agency and the university is informed of the completion for their records. Private property prices within the geographic area around the university are captured by monitoring RSS feeds from property companies.

7   Applying LEAP to the Case Study

Section 4 has shown a detailed, but simple example of using LEAP for architecture alignment. The example shows how LEAP is used to capture the top-level information structures and invariants that arise from a business requirement, how LEAP can be used to represent an architecture of interacting components based on existing IT systems, and then how alignment is established through simulation and rigorous argument.

Section 5 has outlined a pragmatic approach to Architecture Alignment that can be based on a range of technologies. This section follows the method using LEAP. Since the case study is quite large we will present an overview and include samples of the implementation where these are illustrative of our approach.

7.1   Step 1: Model Requirements

Figure 11 shows the information model that supports the KIS requirements. The model is taken directly from the LEAP tool that represents the requirements as a single top-level component. Each University has a number of students. Information is maintained on the cost of both University owned accommodation and private accommodation in the area. A student studies a course and optionally completes an NSS return in their third year of study; the NSS form allows students to comment on the quality of the University's provision of teaching and learning in terms of questions such as: '*Do you agree that you receive prompt feedback on formative assessments?*'.

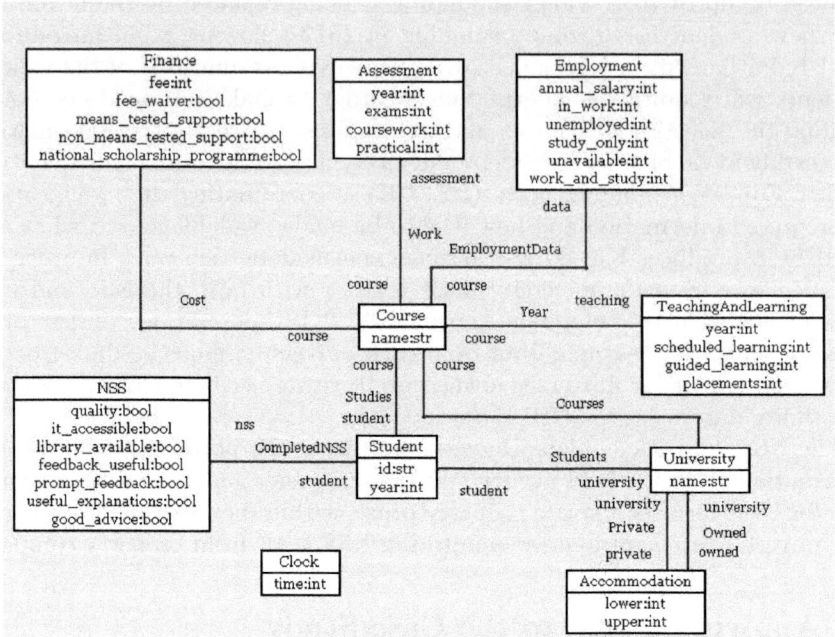

Fig. 11. KIS Information Structure

Each course is delivered in terms of scheduled, guided and practical teaching and learning components, and assessed in terms of exams, courseworks and practicals. Information is maintained nationally about employment statistics for particular courses, such as the salary of graduates and the percentage who are in work or unemployed 6 months after graduation. Each HE course in the UK has a cost and may involve various forms of financial support.

7.2   Step 2: Define L-EA and Simulation

Figure 12 shows the outline of the logical architecture simulator. All component structure in the architecture has been flattened and has been represented as information. For example, in the physical architecture we will be required to implement components for universities and for HEFCE.

The logical architecture will also contain a number of invariants that must be maintained when the logical architecture is refined to become a physical architecture. For example, the values of various fields must be unique and percentage values must add up to 100. The most important invariant that follows from the business requirement is that when the time reaches a specific point, all the information necessary to construct the KIS report must be available. Given this requirement, any mapping from logical to physical must provide KIS data no matter how distributed the data becomes.

```
component kis_logical {
  component kis {
    model { // KIS Information Structure... }
    port in[in]:interface {
      make_university(name:str,courses:void):void;
      register_student(university:str,student:str,course:str):void;
      accommodation(university:str,lower:int,upper:int):void;
      owned(university:str,lower:int,upper:int):void;
      complete_nss(student:str,quality:bool,it_accessible:bool,library_available:bool,...):void
    }
    operations {
      make_university(name,courses) {
        let u = new University(name)
        in for Course(course_name,t1,t2,t3,a1,a2,a3,employment,finance) in courses {
          let c = new Course(course_name)
          in // create and link instances of the information model...
        }
      }
      register_student(university,student,course) {
        find u=University(university) in state {
          find Courses(u,Course(course)) in state {
            let s = new Student(student)
            in new Students(u,s), new Studies(s,Course(course))
          } else error('no course ' + course)
        } else error('no university ' + university)
      }
      complete_nss(student,q,i,l,f,p,u,g) { ... }
      accommodation(university,lower,upper) { ... }
      owned(university,lower,upper) { ... }
    }
  }
  state {
    Time(0)
    Message(0,kis.in,'make_university',['middle england',[
      Course('Computer Science', TeachingAndLearning(1,60,40,0),..., Assessment(1,100,0,0),...,
        Employment(20000,50,20,20,10,0), Finance(9000,true,true,true,true))
    ]])
    Message(1,kis.in,'register_student',['middle england','fred','Computer Science'])
    ...
    Message(2,kis.in,'complete_nss',['fred',true,true,true,true,true,true,true])
    Message(3,kis.in,'accommodation',['middle england',500,1000])
    Message(4,kis.in,'owned',['middle england',500,1000])
    ...
    End(100)
  }
  rules {
    send: Time(t) Message(t,p,m,args) { send(p,m,args); delete Message(t,p,m,args) }
    tick: Time(t) not(Message(t,_,_,_)) not(End(t)) { replace Time(t) with Time(t+1) }
  }
}
```

Fig. 12. Logical Architecture Simulation

7.3   Step 3: Collate Physical-EA

The next step of our method involves reviewing the current physical *as-is* system architecture. Most organizations have a systems overview which is used as the input to this step. The result is an understanding of the current capability of the organization in terms of systems, interfaces, information and events.

The context for the physical EA includes external systems. When generating KIS data, all universities must work with the following external systems: students use the **web** to complete NSS reports; employability information is maintained by the **dhle**; the NSS forms are collated by **nss**; an RSS **property** feed provides information on the cost of accommodation at regular intervals; **hefce** manages the KIS process.

We will use the University of Middlesex (Mdx), London, UK as the basis for our case study. Space limitations prevent us from providing a complete description of the Mdx physical architecture, however it is consistent with most UK HEIs and includes systems for registry, an asset management system that includes a sub-system for university accommodation, an examinations database, a library system, a financial management system called PAFIS, a teaching and learning system called OASIS, an alumni management system, a student portal, and a staff portal.

7.4   Step 4: Configure Physical-EA

The next step of the method analyses the physical system of an organization and takes an appropriate *slice* to produce just those systems that will be involved in the required *to-be* architecture. In the case of supplying KIS data, we know that Mdx will need to provide student, accommodation, teaching and learning, assessment and financial information. Therefore, the P-EA will not include the alumni or library management systems.

7.5   Step 5: Define Physical-EA

Figure 13 shows a physical architecture model for KIS including two universities. The physical architecture distributes the information structures and invariants across multiple components and uses component-nesting within the university components to drill down to particular IT systems. For the purposes of simulation, the multiple universities are constructed using template patterns.

The simulation is driven by the `hefce` component that triggers an event when it is time to construct the KIS reports. The simulation uses pattern matching across multiple events within `hefce` to determine when all of the information has been received as shown in figure 14. Of particular interest are the rules defined by `hefce`. When both registration events are received in any order from NSS and DHLE then `hefce` registers the university. The `kis_run` rule detects when it is time for KIS reporting and sends messages to all universities, to DHLE and to NSS. The replies from these messages are received in an arbitrary order and update the `hefce` database; the `kis` rule detects when updates have occurred (again in any order) and creates the KIS report for each university.

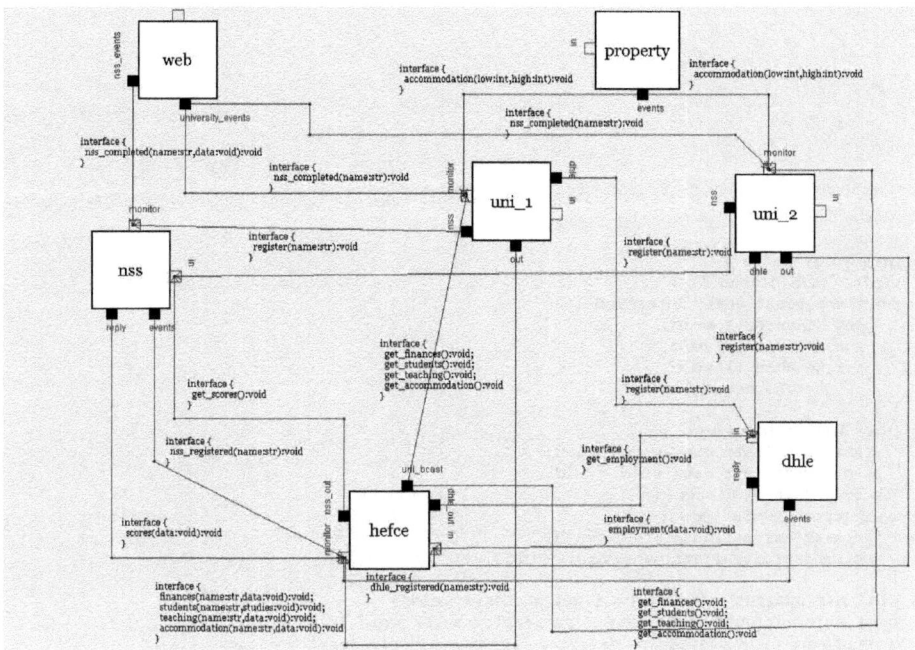

Fig. 13. Physical Architecture

7.6 Step 6: Conformance

Our EA design method produces both a logical and a physical architecture description using the LEAP simulation language. The logical architecture describes what is required and the physical *to-be* architecture defines how existing systems can be used to satisfy the requirements. It remains to validate the physical architecture by showing that the behaviour aligns to the requirements.

In general, conformance can be established using a number of approaches. The context defines a collection of system executions in terms of messages, events and state changes. It is possible to use inspection-based techniques to show that all required executions are handled appropriately by the physical architecture.

Our KIS physical architecture simulation model included Mdx IT systems that managed information on students, finance, property and academic teaching and learning. The invariants for the logical model were translated into equivalent conditions over the physical architecture.

The logical architecture simulation was driven using a sequence of messages that registered courses, registered students, completed NSS forms, and provided property prices. The same messages were used to drive the physical architecture and the results were observed using the LEAP tooling. Figure 15 shows part of the output where LEAP produces HTML. The simulation proceeds by generating clock ticks in response to button clicks. The simulation output shows KIS data rendered as a collection of gui components including a pie-chart and a histogram.

```
component hefce {
  state { KIS_Census(5) }
  port uni_bcast[out]: interface {
      get_finances():void;
      get_students():void;
      get_teaching():void;
      get_accommodation():void
  }
  port in[in]:interface {
    finances(uni:str,data:void):void;
    students(uni:str,data:void):void;
    scores(data:void):void;
    employment(data:void):void;
    teaching(uni:str,data:void):void;
    accommodation(uni:str,data:void):void
  }
  port nss_out[out]: interface { get_scores():void }
  port dhle_out[out]: interface { get_employment():void }
  operations { // updates to database corresponding to input messages ... }
  rules {
    university: NSS_Registered(name) DHLE_Registered(name) { new University(name) }
    kis_run: Time(n) KIS_Census(n) {
      uni_bcast <- get_finances();
      uni_bcast <- get_students();
      uni_bcast <- get_teaching();
      uni_bcast <- get_accommodation();
      dhle_out <- get_employment();
      nss_out <- get_scores()
    }
    kis: University(name)
         Students(name,studies)
         Finance(name,finance)
         Teaching(name,tdata)
         Accommodation(name,adata)
         NSS(data)
         Employment(edata) {
      let filtered_nss = [ nss_data | NSS(student_name,nss_data)        <- data,
                                      Studies(Student(student_name),_) <- studies ];
         filtered_employment = [ Employment(c,d) | Employment(name,c,d) <- edata ]
      in // construct report
    }
  }
}
```

Fig. 14. The HEFCE Simulation

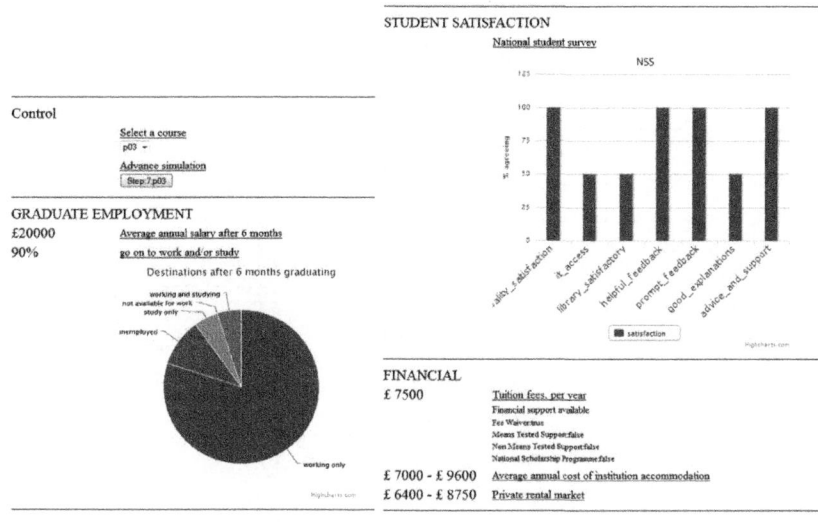

Fig. 15. Part of the KIS Simulation Output

In all cases, no invariants were violated and the output from the logical and physical simulations was identical.

Finally, if we require total confidence in conformance then we need to resort to formal methods such as model checking and theory proving. For large systems such as those found in EA, formal methods are often impractical in terms of complexity. That said, a formal semantics for LEAP is an area for future development in order to investigate whether formal methods could help.

8   Discussion and Further Work

Enterprise Architecture remains a confusing and constantly evolving collection of methods and frameworks which are generally characterized by an expansive outlook, lack of precision, a focus on diagrams and an emphasis on document management. The result is that existing approaches are difficult to analyze and process. This paper has presented an effort to pin down important EA use cases of managing change and better understanding the impact of changing requirements on existing technical architectures of an organization.

We have proposed a synthetic language for EA called LEAP and contrasted it with a leading analytic language called ArchiMate. Our claim is that the large collection of EA features in ArchiMate are not orthogonal and can be mapped to a much smaller collection in LEAP. This claim is validated through a real-world case study although it remains as further work to compare the resulting LEAP simulation with the equivalent ArchiMate models. Furthermore, we do not claim that analytic languages such as ArchiMate are redundant since they

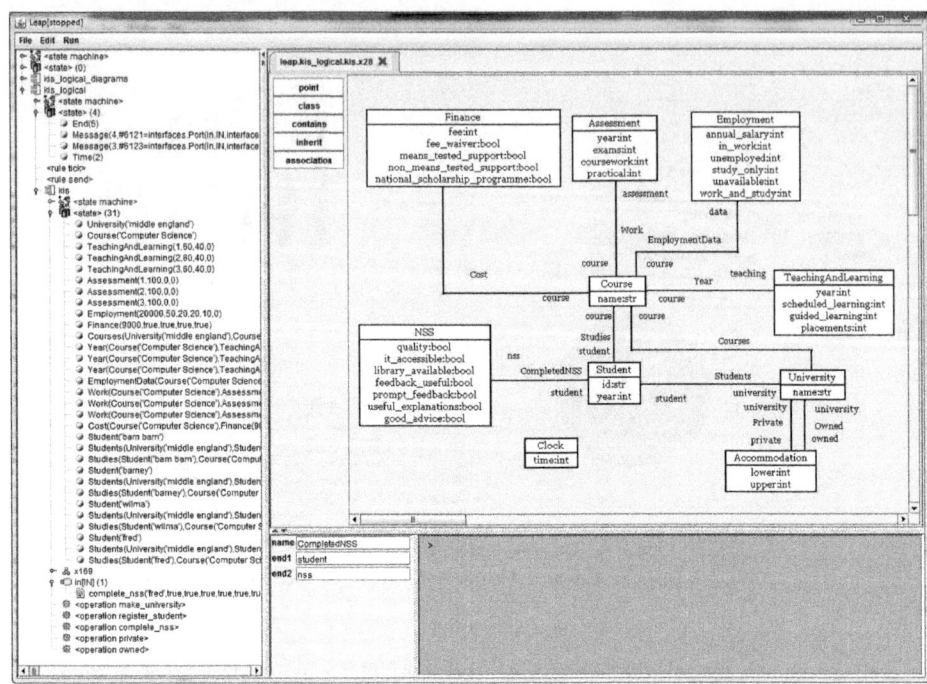

Fig. 16. Leap Tool

are domain-specific and present features in terms recognizable to a business analyst; however, LEAP could be used as a basis for EA language precision through mappings such as that described in table 1. In this way the broad EA could be captured by ArchiMate and then simulated and analysed using LEAP by making decisions about how each ArchiMate concept maps onto elements in LEAP and by introducing procedural and structural detail where required. Simulation results and analysis performed in terms of LEAP can then be presented back to the analyst using corresponding ArchiMate concepts.

It remains to show that the features of LEAP are necessary and sufficient for EA construction and analysis. Our primary concern in this paper is to provide examples of LEAP *in action* for simulation and to show that an operational semantics leads to scope for analysis that is more rigorous than that supported by other methods. Our guiding principle for the definition of LEAP features has been providing a *synthetic* language for EA by identifying low-level precisely defined concepts that can be freely combined. LEAP allows an organization to be modelled as a single component or as a highly-structured collection of collaborative service-oriented and event-based components. An organization can be modelled multiple times from different perspectives and the relationships can be analysed, thereby providing scope for step-wise refinement and a route to reconfiguration including migration to a SOA-based architecture. As such, we claim that LEAP is highly expressive, but more empirical work is required to establish the claim that it is both necessary and sufficient.

Our claim goes further by proposing that EA languages should be executable wherever that makes sense. EA aims to address features of organizations; organizations are systems that *operate* in terms of structure, resources and information. LEAP provides a simple and universal basis for representing these EA characteristic features without introducing unnecessary distinctions between otherwise fundamentally identical concepts. This claim has been validated by applying LEAP to a real-world EA case study in order to address a typical EA use-case: Architecture-Alignment. We have shown that an operational semantics can be used in a practical sense to build confidence that two different architectural descriptions of the same system are equivalent.

We claim that LEAP represents a contribution to industrial EA because it takes a pragmatic approach to introducing precision in EA. Current EA languages lie at the *sketching* end of the development life-cycle. This is valuable, but is not amenable to automated analysis. At the other end of the spectrum lies formal methods and their associated tools, however it is not clear that there is any evidence that such a formalized approach to EA would be tractable given the size and complexity of the systems involved. LEAP lies in-between on this spectrum by supporting diagrams for the key features of an architecture, a high-level programming language for the details and a semantics that, in principle, does not rule out formal analysis in the future.

How would Industry use LEAP? Our experience with KIS and other case studies we have developed, is that the ability to create a simulation of part of an organization is very valuable. LEAP does not require components to map on to physical resources and organizational units, it is intended that features of an EA application, whether tangible or intangible, can be expressed in terms of components, data, rules, operations, constraints, state-machines, and messages. A novel feature of LEAP is that both components and operations are higher-order which means that it is easy to capture template patterns, as shown in the case of the tills in the greengrocer example and the universities in the KIS case study. In another example not reported here, we have used template patterns to capture the life-cycle of a customer record as a component.

Therefore, Industry can use LEAP to produce simulations of architectures at any level of abstraction, and the operational nature of LEAP makes it practical to compare the same system developed to different levels of detail. Since the information is represented as LEAP models, it is possible to generate artifacts from them, including code, although this is something to be investigated as future work. In addition, since components are encapsulated, our intention is to allow LEAP to interface to existing systems, thereby providing a means to migrate an existing architecture by simulating the new components and gradually replacing them with new IT systems.

Our use of LEAP for the KIS analysis at Mdx has shown that existing University information systems can support the new HEFCE regulations subject to being able to provide the appropriate interfaces and supporting the information models defined in the simulation. Given a simulation, the mapping from LEAP to real information systems is straightforward. LEAP tooling supports single stepping through the simulation together with snapshots of the simulation state as shown in figure 16.

LEAP does not claim to be a universal technology for EA, however, as described above, we have taken a fundamentally different approach to the design of a language for EA compared to that provided by current systems. Since LEAP is a synthetic language it is necessarily limited, however it provides a basis on which to test the hypothesis that the our proposed concepts are sufficient for a wide variety of EA use-cases and, where it is found lacking, our claim is that the required extensions will be orthogonal and precisely defined where possible. Current limitations include the ability to express and manage the refinement of business goals and to express non-functional system requirements (such as cost and risk). We have started a process of consultation with Industry in order to understand how these features need to be represented and processed.

References

1. Arsanjani, A., Ghosh, S., Allam, A., Abdollah, T., Ganapathy, S., Holley, K.: Soma: A method for developing service-oriented solutions. IBM Systems Journal 47(3), 377–396 (2008)
2. Assmann, M., Engels, G.: Transition to Service-Oriented Enterprise Architecture. In: Morrison, R., Balasubramaniam, D., Falkner, K. (eds.) ECSA 2008. LNCS, vol. 5292, pp. 346–349. Springer, Heidelberg (2008)
3. Biggs, B.: Ministry of defence architectural framework (modaf). IEE Seminar Digests 43 (2005)
4. Bucher, T., Fischer, R., Kurpjuweit, S., Winter, R.: Analysis and application scenarios of enterprise architecture: An exploratory study. In: 10th IEEE International Enterprise Distributed Object Computing Conference Workshops, EDOCW 2006 (2006)
5. Buhr, R.J.A., Casselman, R.S.O.: Use case maps for object-oriented systems, vol. 302. Prentice Hall (1996)
6. Chan, Y.E., Reich, B.H.: IT alignment: what have we learned? Journal of Information Technology 22(4), 297–315 (2007)
7. Cheesman, J., Daniels, J.: UML components. Addison-Wesley (2001)
8. D'Souza, D.F., Wills, A.C.: Objects, components, and frameworks with UML: the catalysis approach. Addison-Wesley Longman Publishing Co., Inc., Boston (1999)
9. Ekstedt, M., Johnson, P., Lindstrom, A., Gammelgard, M., Johansson, E., Plaza-ola, L., Silva, E., Lilieskold, J.: Consistent enterprise software system architecture for the cio - a utility-cost based approach. In: Proceedings of the 37th Annual Hawaii International Conference on System Sciences, HICSS 2004 (2004)
10. Frank, U.: Multi-perspective enterprise modeling (memo) conceptual framework and modeling languages. In: Proceedings of the 35th Annual Hawaii International Conference on System Sciences, HICSS 2002, pp. 1258–1267. IEEE (2002)

11. Goethals, F.G., Snoeck, M., Lemahieu, W., Vandenbulcke, J.: Management and enterprise architecture click: The fad (e) e framework. Information Systems Frontiers 8(2), 67–79 (2006)
12. The Open Group. Archimate technical standard (2008), http://www.opengroup.org/archimate/
13. Henderson, J.C., Venkatraman, N.: Strategic alignment: Leveraging information technology for transforming organizations. IBM Systems Journal 32(1) (1993)
14. Huemer, C., Liegl, P., Motal, T., Schuster, R., Zapletal, M.: The development process of the un/cefact modeling methodology. In: Proceedings of the 10th International Conference on Electronic Commerce, p. 36. ACM (2008)
15. ITU. Basic reference model of open distributed processing - part 1: Overview and guide to use. ITU Recommendation X.901 | ISO/IEC 10746-1. ISO/ITU (1994)
16. Johnson, P., Johansson, E., Sommestad, T., Ullberg, J.: A tool for enterprise architecture analysis. In: 11th IEEE International Enterprise Distributed Object Computing Conference, EDOC 2007, pp. 142–142. IEEE (2007)
17. Johnson, P., Lagerström, R., Närman, P., Simonsson, M.: Enterprise architecture analysis with extended influence diagrams. Information Systems Frontiers 9(2) (2007)
18. Lankhorst, M.: Introduction to enterprise architecture. In: Enterprise Architecture at Work. The Enterprise Engineering Series. Springer, Heidelberg (2009)
19. Michelson, B.M.: Event-driven architecture overview. Patricia Seybold Group (2006)
20. Niemann, K.D.: From enterprise architecture to IT governance: elements of effective IT management. Vieweg+ Teubner Verlag (2006)
21. Ould, M.A.: Business Process Management: a rigorous approach. British Informatics Society Ltd. (2005)
22. Overbeek, S., Klievink, B., Janssen, M.: A flexible, event-driven, service-oriented architecture for orchestrating service delivery. IEEE Intelligent Systems 24(5), 31–41 (2009)
23. Pereira, C.M., Sousa, P.: A method to define an enterprise architecture using the zachman framework. In: Proceedings of the 2004 ACM Symposium on Applied Computing, pp. 1366–1371. ACM (2004)
24. Raymond, K.: Reference model of open distributed processing (rm-odp): Introduction. In: IFIP TC6 International Conference on Open Distributed Processing, pp. 3–14. Chapman and Hall, Brisbane (1995)
25. Riege, C., Aier, S.: A Contingency Approach to Enterprise Architecture Method Engineering. In: Feuerlicht, G., Lamersdorf, W. (eds.) ICSOC 2008. LNCS, vol. 5472, pp. 388–399. Springer, Heidelberg (2009)
26. Sharon, G., Etzion, O.: Event-processing network model and implementation. IBM Systems Journal 47(2), 321–334 (2008)
27. Spencer, J., et al.: TOGAF Enterprise Edition Version 8.1 (2004)
28. Steen, M.W.A., Strating, P., Lankhorst, M.M., ter Doest, H., Iacob, M.E.: Service-oriented enterprise architecture. In: Stojanovic, Z., Dahanayake, A. (eds.) Service Oriented Systems Engineering, Hershey, pp. 132–154 (2005)
29. Tang, A., Han, J., Chen, P.: A comparative analysis of architecture frameworks. In: 11th Asia-Pacific Software Engineering Conference, 2004, pp. 640–647. IEEE (2004)
30. Wegmann, A., Balabko, P., Lê, L.S., Regev, G., Rychkova, I.: A method and tool for business-it alignment in enterprise architecture. In: CAiSE 2005 Forum. Citeseer (2005)

31. Wegmann, A., Regev, G., Rychkova, I., Lê, L.S., De La Cruz, J.D., Julia, P.: Business and it alignment with seam for enterprise architecture. In: 11th IEEE International Enterprise Distributed Object Computing Conference, EDOC 2007, p. 111. IEEE (2007)
32. Wirfs-Brock, R., Wilkerson, B., Wiener, L.: Designing object-oriented software, vol. 13. Prentice Hall, Englewood Cliffs (1990)
33. Wisnosky, D.E., Vogel, J.: DoDAF Wizdom: A Practical Guide to Planning, Managing and Executing Projects to Build Enterprise Architectures Using the Department of Defense Architecture Framework, DoDAF (2004)
34. Zachman, J.A.: A framework for information systems architecture. IBM Systems Journal 38(2/3) (1999)

A Practice-Based Framework for Enterprise Coherence*

Roel Wagter[1,3], H.A. (Erik) Proper[2,3], and Dirk Witte[4]

[1] Ordina, Nieuwegein, The Netherlands
[2] PRC Henri Tudor, Luxembourg
[3] Radboud University Nijmegen, Nijmegen, The Netherlands
[4] Logica, Amstelveen, The Netherlands
roel.wagter@ordina.nl, erik.proper@tudor.lu,
dirk.witte@logica.com

Abstract. In this paper, the authors discuss a practice-based framework that enables enterprises to make the coherence between key aspects, such as business and IT, explicit. The term "coherence" is preferred over the more common term "alignment", since the latter is generally associated with bringing two concepts in line (typically "Business" and "IT"). The word coherence, however, stresses the need to go beyond this. Enterprise coherence considers the alignment of *all* important aspects of an enterprise.

The core driver for the development of the Enterprise Coherence Framework (ECF), as presented in this paper, was the costly failure of many (large scale) enterprise transformation projects. These resulted in the initiation of the GEA (General Enterprise Architecting) multi-client research programme, involving twenty client organizations. This, still ongoing, research programme started in 2006. The current focus of the programme's efforts is on the continuous evaluation and further improvement of the programme's results. One of the core results of the GEA research programme is the Enterprise Coherence Framework (ECF), which enables a more explicit reasoning about the coherence between the relevant aspects of an enterprise. This framework, on its turn, enables the deliberate governance of enterprise coherence.

In this paper, both the practical and theoretical roots of the framework will be discussed, as well as experiences in its use in real world settings.

Keywords: business-IT alignment, enterprise coherence, enterprise architecture.

1 Introduction

Efforts to transform an enterprise, from its business processes to the underlying IT, often fail. In Op't Land et al. [1], the authors provide a summary of possible causes for failures of strategic initiatives: "*The road from strategy formulation to strategy execution, including the use of programmatic steering, is certainly not an easy one to travel. Research shows that less than 60% of the strategic objectives in organizations are reached.*" In addition, our own experiences[1] with enterprise transformations in

---

* This work has been partially sponsored by the *Fonds National de la Recherche Luxembourg* (www.fnr.lu), via the PEARL programme.

[1] The authors either currently work for a consultancy firm, or have worked for one in the past. As part of their daily work, they have been involved in several large enterprise transformations.

E. Proper et al. (Eds.): PRET 2012, LNBIP 120, pp. 77–95, 2012.

practice, also indicate that existing methods and frameworks for enterprise architecture often fail to contribute to the success of such transformation projects.

As argued in [1,2], architecture should offer senior management the means to obtain insight, and to make decisions about the direction of enterprise transformations. As such, it should act as a means to steer enterprise transformations, while in particular enable senior management to govern coherence. In our view, existing approaches and frameworks, such as, Zachman [3], DYA [4], Abcouwer [5], Henderson & Venkatraman [6], TOGAF [7], IAF [8], ArchiMate [9,10], take an "engineering oriented" style of communicating with senior management and stakeholders in general. The architecture frameworks underlying each of these approaches are very much driven by "engineering principles", and as such correspond to a Blue-print style of thinking about change [11]. To act as a steering instrument for senior management, a Blue-print style of thinking, however, does not suffice. Stakeholder interests, formal and informal power structures within enterprises, and the associated processes of creating win-win situations and forming coalitions, should also be taken into consideration. In terms of De Caluwé [11], this is more the Yellow-print style of thinking about change.

In 2006, these experiences and insights triggered the consultancy firm Ordina to initiate a multi-client research programme (www.groeiplatformgea.nl), resulting in the development of the GEA (General Enterprise Architecting) method [12,2]. As a prelude to the actual start of the programme, a survey was conducted among the participating organizations to identify the requirements on the desired outcome of the programme. This survey showed that these experiences were not limited to Ordina only, but was shared among a broad range of client organizations participating in the programme[2]. The underlying issues were also considered grave enough for the participating client organizations to indeed co-invest, in terms of time and money, in the GEA research programme.

The core result of the GEA research programme is the GEA method [2]. In the research programme, this method was developed based on several case studies with the client organizations participating in the programme, using a combination of design science [13] as the overall rhythm and case study research [14] to leverage the findings from the case studies (see for example [15]). In its current form, the GEA method comprises of three core ingredients [2]. Next to the Enterprise Coherence Assessment (ECA) that allows organizations to assess their ability to govern coherence during enterprise transformation, it contains an Enterprise Coherence Framework (ECF) and a (situational) Enterprise Coherence Governance (ECG) approach. The latter includes the identification of specific deliverables to produced/results, processes needed to produce these deliverables/results, as well as an articulation of the responsibilities and competences of the people involved. The ECF, which is the focus of this paper, enables en-

---

[2] During different stages of the GEA research programme, the following client organizations were involved: ABN AMRO; ANWB; Achmea; Belastingdienst - Centrum voor ICT; ICTU; ING; Kappa Holding; Ministerie van Binnenlandse Zaken en Koninkrijksrelaties; Ministerie van Defensie; Ministerie van Justitie - Dienst Justitiële Inrichtingen; Ministerie van LNV - Dienst Regelingen; Ministerie van Landbouw, Natuur en Voedselkwaliteit; Nederlandse Spoorwegen; PGGM; Politie Nederland; Prorail; Provincie Flevoland; Rabobank; Rijkswaterstaat; UWV; Wehkamp.

terprises to set up their own *coherence dashboard* in terms of the enterprise coherence can be governed/improved during enterprise transformations. This, enterprise specific, dashboard enables senior management to govern the coherence between key aspects of an enterprise during a transformations.

The remainder of this paper is structured as follows. In Section 2, we provide a short background to the GEA research programme. Section 3 then briefly summarizes the requirements on the results of the GEA programme (and the Enterprise Coherence Framework (ECF) in particular). Section 4, 5 and 6 then discuss the actual ECF in three steps, covering the level of organizational *purpose*, the *design* level, and the *connections* between these levels respectively. In our discussions of the framework, we will include experiences/examples from real world case studies conducted at the client organizations involved in the GEA programme.

2 Background to the Research Programme

As mentioned before, the GEA research programme started with an initial survey among the participating client organizations. This initial survey indicated that a lack of coherence between different aspects of the enterprise, before, during, and after, transformations as a key cause for the failures. It also indicated the necessity to go beyond the traditional Business-IT alignment thinking as e.g. advocated in the classical paper by Henderson & Venkatraman [6]. As a result of the initial survey, the GEA programme continued with the working hypothesis: *the overall performance of an enterprise is positively influenced by a strong coherence among the key aspects of the enterprise, including business processes, organizational culture, product portfolio, human resources, information systems, IT support, etc.*. GEA refers to this coherence as *enterprise coherence* [12,2]. The GEA project partners preferred this term over the term "Business-IT alignment", as the latter would suggest as if "only" business and IT would need to be aligned. Enterprise coherence, however, stresses the need to go beyond this, and align all important aspects of an enterprise. More recent sources also explicitly acknowledge/indicate the need for enterprise architecture methods to look well beyond the traditional Business-to-IT stack, consider for example: [16,17,18].

To validate the role of coherence in the failure of transformations, a first step in the GEA programme was the development of the Enterprise Coherence Assessment (ECA) [19]. The ECA allowed us to obtain a clearer understanding of enterprise coherence, as well as the impact of adequate governance of enterprise coherence on the success of transformations. After applying this assessment to the organizations involved in the GEA programme, it was found that more than 80% of the participating organizations lack a deliberate governance of their enterprise coherence, while the lack of coherence had a negative impact on the success of the transformations [19]. A report [20] produced by the (Dutch) General Court of Auditors, on the failures on IT projects in the public sector, also corroborates these findings. In this report, the lack of coherence between several aspects is identified as a key cause in the failure of these projects.

Consequently, it became the core goal of the GEA programme to find/develop instruments to make enterprise coherence explicit enough to reason about it in a specific organization, and develop associated processes to allow it to be governed. An overview, aimed at practitioners, of the results of the first iterations of this research programme has been reported in [2][3]. To the partners of the GEA programme, this clearly demonstrated the need for further research into governance of enterprise coherence. More specifically, the GEA programme [2] adopted the following research objectives:

1. Definition of the core indicators and factors influencing and/or defining enterprise coherence.
2. Identification of the impact of enterprise coherence on the organizational performance.
3. An instrument to assess an enterprise's level of coherence.
4. Instruments to guard/improve the level of coherence in enterprises during transformations.

The outcomes of the ECA studies were also used to gather more specific requirements on the GEA method. These initial requirements were complemented, using desk research, by requirements originating from three relevant other fields: management control [21], system theory [22,23] and strategic change [24]. More details on these requirements can be found in [2]. In the further (still ongoing) development of the GEA method, the design science method [13] was/is used as the overarching "rhythm" of the research project, combined with case study research [14] to evaluate the application of the different iterations of the GEA method.

The current version of the GEA method [2] was already refined based on several case studies with the client organizations participating in the programme. In its current form, the GEA method comprises of three core ingredients [2]. Next to the Enterprise Coherence Assessment (ECA) that allows organizations to assess their ability to govern coherence during enterprise transformation, it contains an Enterprise Coherence Framework (ECF) and a (situational) Enterprise Coherence Governance (ECG) approach. The latter includes the identification of specific deliverables to produced/results, processes needed to produce these deliverables/results, as well as an articulation of the responsibilities and competences of the people involved. The ECF, which is the focus of this paper, enables enterprise to set up their own *coherence dashboard* in terms of the enterprise coherence can be governed/improved during enterprise transformations. This, enterprise specific, dashboard enables senior management to govern the coherence between key aspects of an enterprise during a transformations.

3   Requirements on the Governance of Enterprise Coherence

Based on the triggers that lead to the initiation of the GEA programme, an initial survey was held among the members of the GEA programme to gather requirements on the governance of enterprise coherence. Based on these requirements, a first theoretical framework to explicitly reason about an enterprise's coherence was developed. This initial version of the ECF was then evolved further, based on its use in practice. In

---

[3] For strategic reason, the initial target of the results was the Dutch language community, as most participating organizations where also based in the Dutch language area. In the near future, these initial results will be made available in English as well.

doing so, the GEA programme used the multiple case study research approach (see Yin [14]). More details concerning the way we applied the case study approach in the GEA programme can be found in [19].

The first version of the ECF also allowed us to develop the Enterprise Coherence Assessment (ECA). The application of the (first version of the) ECA in the participating organizations, also resulted in further requirements towards the ECF and ECG. The resulting requirements are shown in Table 1.

Since the governance of enterprise coherence should be part of the overall organizational governance, this initial set of requirements was strengthened by augmenting it with insights from other areas relevant to organizational governance in general: management control, systems theory, and strategic change.

One of the leading approaches in the world of management control concerns the work of Simons on the *"Levers of Control"* [21]. Inspired by these levers of control the additional requirements listed in Table 2 were formulated.

The second foundation concerns the open system theory in which the organization is seen as an open system [22,23]. Within the framework of the framework formulated in this control paradigm a set of conditions for effective control has been formulated. Compliance with these conditions also implies a promise, namely to achieve an effective control situation. Inspired by these conditions for effective control we derived the additional requirements as shown in Table 3.

The third foundation for GEA is based on the notion that organizations are a social-technical system involving humans and technology. In deriving additional requirements for the GEA programme, we based ourselves on the work of Balogun, et al. [24] on *"Exploring Strategic Change"*. The basic principle is that every choice made in a change process should be based on the context and the purpose of the change process. A study conducted in 2004 by Deloitte & Touche *"What is the best change approach"* [25] enhanced this basic idea with the statement that there is a link between the choice of approach and purpose of the change. Inspired by these insights we derived the additional requirements as listed in Table 4.

At the end of the requirements gathering process, we were able to establish the basic philosophy of GEA. As mentioned before, in this philosophy we took the following hypothesis as a starting point: *the overall performance of an enterprise is positively influenced by a strong cohesion among the key aspects of the enterprise, including business processes, organizational culture, product portfolio, human resources, information systems, IT support, etc.* Taking this hypothesis as a starting point, gave us the following insights. When presuming the hypothesis is true, it is natural to take the view that enterprise coherence is indeed an important issue. An issue that organizations need to deliberately influence and govern. To govern coherence one needs the levers to adjust the coherence and to be able to do this one has to be able to reason explicitly about it.

Taking our definition of coherence into account, and the fact that organizations are "living" organisms, also produces the insight that coherence has a fluid character (i.e. it changes on its own accord) which implies that the governance should be carried out on a permanent base. These insights triggered the question *"by which phenomena, and when, is the coherence of the enterprise improved or decreased?"*. Coherence will especially be influenced at the moment an organization needs to answer/meet major business

Table 1. Requirements after the initial survey and applying the ECA

Success factor	Requirement
Strategy driven	1) It is necessary to take the concerns, and associated strategic dialogues, of senior management as a starting point.
Social forces	2) The social forces within an enterprise, be they of political, informal, or cultural nature, should be a leading element in governing enterprise coherence.
EA Vision	3) One must have an EA vision in order to be able to establish EA as a business value driver and make explicit how coherence contributes to both the image and opinion formation phases of the decision making process and must closely resemble and simulate the way of thinking. One prerequisite is that the top of the organization firmly holds this EA vision.
Commitment	4) The added value of EA as a governance tool should be recognized and promoted by all parties concerned. Also the added value of EA compared with other control tools that are in use.
Organization	5) To establish the EA function an integral approach to vision development, processes, products, people and resources needed for EA is necessary.
Customization	6) EA is a flexible concept, which means that the number and character of organizational angles to govern the enterprise and their associated relationships depend on the situation.
Customer orientation	7) The EA processes and products should support the control processes of the enterprise in a tailor made way, by supplying the necessary results supporting these control processes.
Scope	8) EA moves at a strategic level and gives direction in decision making on tactical and operational levels by means of lines of policy and must be done in an independent way to include all angles at stake in decision making processes.
Product distinction	9) From the point of accessibility and understanding it is necessary to distinguish between EA management products and EA specialist products. This means that it is possible to communicate with the right target groups and with the right EA products.
Resource allocation	10) Management must provide the EA function with people with the necessary competencies, time, budget and other resources for EA to realize the added value of EA.
Participation	11) Enterprise architects must participate in the organization's governance processes and must have direct access to managers on a peer to peer basis.
Direction	12) The EA governance products must provide direction to change programmes and the existing organization.
Completeness	13) A complete and coherent set of organizational angles must be brought together by the decision makers.
Permanence	14) EA must be arranged as a continuous process whereby coherence is permanently adjusted to the dynamics of the internal and external environment.
Event driven	15) EA must be applied as a governance instrument at the moment major business issues arise in order to establish integral solutions and approaches on time.

Table 2. Requirements originating from the management control framework [21]

Lever of control	Requirement
Diagnostic control systems	1) Goals have to be an element of enterprise coherence at the level of organizational purpose, and objectives must be an element of enterprise coherence at the design level of an organization.
Belief systems	2) The level of purpose of the organization must be within the scope of EA. This requirement is associated with the previous mentioned requirement "scope".
Boundary systems	3) Boundaries must be made explicit since boundaries define relations between angles of an organization, and as such form a basic asset of enterprise coherence.
Interactive control systems	4) The effect of intended strategic interventions on the enterprise coherence should be made clear interactively and beforehand.

Table 3. Requirements originating from the open systems theory [22,23]

Conditions for effective control	Requirement
Specify a goal to the controlled system	1) Objectives have to be an element of enterprise coherence at the design level of an organization. (This requirement is also posed by the framework of management control, see Table 2.)
Have a model of the controlled system	2) The model of enterprise coherence must represent the dynamics of the design level of an organization.
Have information about the controlled system	3) The actual state of enterprise coherence must be represented on a permanent basis including current state as well as future directions.
Have sufficient control variety	4) Enterprise coherence governance must have sufficient levers to influence enterprise coherence on the design level and support the interdependancy with the level of purpose as well, including: forward and backward governance, event driven and cyclic governance, single and multi level governance (recursivity and projection).
Have sufficient information processing capacity	5) Restrict the complexity and information overload by differentiating enterprise coherence in several interdependent levels. Allocate sufficient resources to enterprise coherence governance, distinguished by processes, products, people, means, governance, methodology and all based on an vision.

issues. Therefore, the governance of enterprise coherence must be an integral part of, and significantly contribute to, the processes of formulating answers to the major business issues. Using coherence governance in these processes leads to integral solutions and approaches, and ultimately to a permanent improvement/maintenance of the organizational coherence.

Table 4. Requirements originating from the strategic change framework [24]

Socio-technical combinations	Requirement
Choice made in a change process should be based on the context and the purpose	1) The scope of enterprise coherence governance should include both internal and external angles of the organizational transaction environment. 2) The purpose of a change process should be in line with the goals on the level of purpose and the objectives on the design level. 3) The organizational aspects that are dominant in the solution for a business problem, determine the choice of approach. 4) Every change process should be argued by the application of the enterprise coherence governance before execution.
Choice of an appropriate approach determines the success	5) The "solution direction and choice of approach" should be just one element of decision. 6) Regarding the decision making process, enterprise coherence governance should contribute to both the solution direction and choice of approach of a business issue. 7) Enterprise coherence governance should guide the realization of the "solution direction and choice of approach" of a business issue. 8) An appropriate approach needs appropriate enterprise coherence products.

4 Enterprise Coherence at the Level of Organizational Purpose

As mentioned before, the ECF distinguishes three areas of coherence: coherence at the level of organizational purpose, coherence at the design level of the organization and coherence between these levels. Figure 1 provides a summary of the ECF. The different elements of the ECF will be elaborated upon in this section, and the next section. In this section we focus on coherence at the strategic level, while the next two sections will address the other two areas of coherence.

In general terms, the Enterprise Coherence Framework consists of a set of so called *cohesive elements* and *cohesive relationships* between them. The overall level of cohesion within an actual enterprise is really determined by the explicitness of the cohesive elements, and quality/consistency of the cohesive relationships, in this enterprise. This also allows enterprises to govern their cohesion, in particular by guarding the cohesive relationships. While this may sound abstract, the discussion of the cohesive elements and their relationships as provided in the remainder of this section, and the next two sections, will make this more tangible.

At the level of organizational purpose, we essentially adapt the *"Strategic Development Process Model"* as proposed by Kaplan & Norton [26], the *"Strategy Formulation"* approach by Thenmozhi [27] and the notion of endless pursuit of a company's mission from *"Building Your Company's Vision"* by Collins & Porras [28]. Based on these theories we distinguish five key cohesive elements: *Mission, Vision, Core Values, Goals* and *Strategy*:

Mission – the mission is a brief, typically one sentence, statement that defines the fundamental purpose of the organization [26] that is *"enduringly pursued but never*

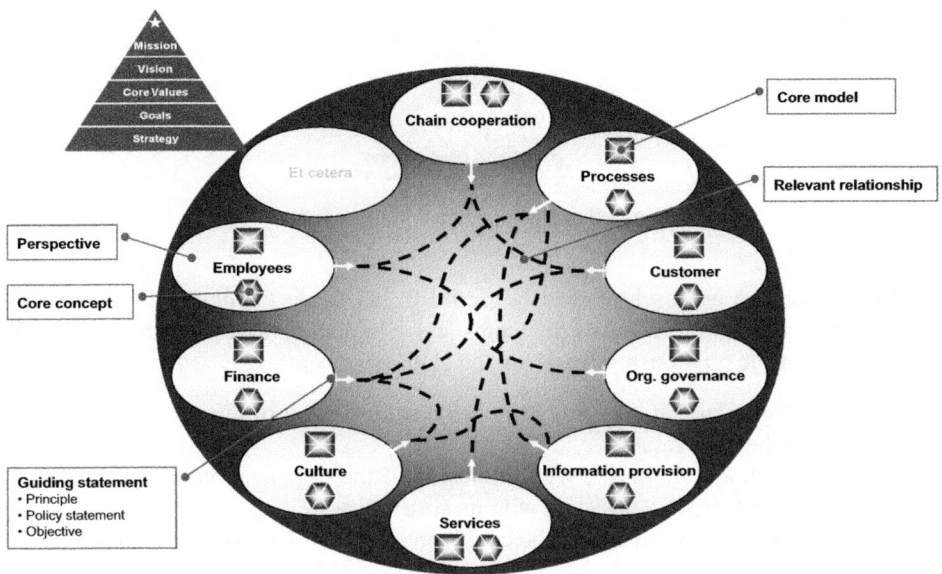

Fig. 1. GEA coherence elements

fulfilled" [28]. It should include what the organization provides to its clients and inform executives and employees about the overall goal they have come together to pursue [26].

Vision – the vision is a concise statement that operationalizes the mission in terms of the mid to long-term goals of the organization. The vision should be external and market oriented and should express – preferably in aspirational terms – how the organization wants to be perceived by the world [26]. Senge [29] indicates that in a vision there must be a creative tension between the present and the enticing imagination of the future and has to show enough ambition, which can be translated into goals and strategies.

Core values – the core values of an organization prescribe its desired behaviour, character and culture [26]. We consider core values as guiding statements at the highest level of sense giving in an organization. Together with the mission, the core values are therefore regarded as most invariant.

Goals – the vision operationalized in terms of concrete goals. These goals acts as success factors in judging the feasibility of strategies. The goals, as success factors, define the desired outcome (short term goals) from successful strategy execution [26].

Strategy – a strategy of an organization forms a comprehensive master plan stating how the organization will pursue its mission. It should also maximize the competitive advantages and minimize competitive disadvantages [27].

These cohesive elements lead to the organizational purpose triangle as depicted in Figure 2.

Fig. 2. The organizational purpose triangle

The coherence at this level can be derived, and made explicit, by the organization's definitions of the cohesive elements and establishing/assessing the consistency and quality of the relationships between the elements:

- The strategies should arguably lead to the achievement of the set goals, while not violating the core values.
- The goals should be in line with the vision of the organization, and ultimately its mission, while being consistent with its core values.
- The core values should at least be consistent with the organization's mission.

To indeed be able to establish/assess the consistency and quality of these cohesive relationships, it is of great importance that an organization's definitions of the elements are indeed available, and are explicit enough. They do constitute the fundamental drivers that shape the enterprise coherence at the design level of the organization. In practice, the elements at the organizational purpose level are often documented in rather broad and informal terms, also increasing the risk of a low level of enterprise coherence at the design level.

5   Enterprise Coherence at the Design Level

At the design level, the organization's strategy is translated into the blue-prints of the operational organization, involving a.o. its business processes, financial flows, logistic flows, human resources, information systems, housing, machines, IT, etc. To achieve enterprise coherence, the coherence at the design level needs to be governed as well. Decision makers need indicators and controls to indeed govern the coherence at this level.

5.1   Perspectives

A distinction between coherence at the level of organizational purpose, and coherence at the level of design, is consistent with the "*Structure follows strategy*" principle from Chandler [30]. This leads to the question *How do we make the enterprise coherence explicit on the design level of the organization?* Since a person is unable to have an in depth overview of the entire organization, let alone to control it, it is necessary to distinguish multiple angles of governance. For the several angles of governance, GEA introduces the cohesive element of "Perspective". In GEA a perspective has been defined as: *an angle from which one wishes to govern/steer/influence enterprise transformations.*

The set of perspectives used in a specific enterprise depend very much on its formal and informal power structures. Both internally, and externally. Typical examples are culture, customer, products/services, business processes, information provision, finance, value chain, corporate governance, etc. In GEA's view, it are really these perspectives that need to be aligned, in order to achieve enterprise coherence.

As an example, Table 5 shows the perspectives that were selected by one of the Dutch Ministries participating in the project. This set of perspectives also illustrates the need to align more aspects of an enterprise rather than just business and IT. Several of the perspectives may put *requirements* towards IT support, *information provisioning* followed by *communication* being the dominant ones in this sense. However, the chosen set of perspectives shows that when it comes to *alignment*, the stakeholders do not think in terms of Business/IT alignment, but in a much refined web of aspects that need alignment.

Table 5. Example definitions of perspectives

Perspective	Definition
Information provisioning	All processes, activities, people and resources for obtaining, processing and delivery of relevant information for our organization.
Collaboration	Collaboration needed to contribute to a common result on the team, entity or organization levels.
Processes	A coherent set of activities needed to deliver results of our organization.
Governance	Influencing our organization such that the desired corporate goals are attained.
Employees	All persons who execute tasks or activities within our organization.
Stakeholders	Legal entities or persons for whom the activities of our organization are important.
Culture	Explicit and implicit norms, values and behaviour within our organization.
Services	All services that our organization, within legal frameworks, or through agreed appointments with statutory authorities, establishes and delivers to customers.
Finance	The planning, acquisition, management and accountability of funds our organization.
Customers	Customers of a service of our organization
Law & regulations	All legal frameworks that form the basis for the task performance of our organization.
Communication	An active process in which information is exchanged between two or more parties or persons, regardless of how that is achieved.

In principle, GEA's concept of perspective is related to the notion of viewpoint as defined in architecture standards such as TOGAF [7] and the IEEE Architecture definition [31]. These concepts are, however, not the same. A perspective is an angle from which one wants to *govern* enterprise transformation. Given the underlying concern of this desire to govern, a viewpoint can be defined that captures the way one wants to view/contemplate the enterprise from this concern. As such, one might say that GEA's notion of perspective could be defined as a "governance viewpoint".

Note again, that GEA takes the stance that the set of perspectives used by a specific enterprise on its *coherence dashboard* is highly organization specific. This set is therefore expected to not correspond to the cells of well known design/engineering frameworks such as Zachman [32], TOGAF's content framework [7] or the Integrated Architecture Framework [8].

5.2   Core Concepts

The practices of the organizations participating in the GEA programme have shown that in general nine to twelve perspectives are identified. The reason for this span (nine to twelve) of perspectives is rooted on the general administrative span of control. In practice, however, we did encountered several situations in which senior management initially wanted to govern the enterprise from far more than twelve angles. In these cases we quite naturally discovered clusters of perspectives with a high correlation, allowing us to compose these perspectives into broader ones. This also led to the realization that another cohesive element was needed: "Core Concepts". A core concept, within a perspective, is defined as: *a concept that plays a key role in governing the organization from that perspective*. In the cases where we were initially confronted with many more than nine perspectives, most of these actually turned out to be the core concepts within more broader defined perspectives.

Examples of core concepts within the perspective of Finance are: "Financing" and "Budgeting". In Table 6, we have listed some of the core concepts that are relevant to one of the Dutch Ministries participating in the GEA programme.

Table 6. Example core concepts

Information provision	Processes	Governance	Stakeholders
Digitization	Time and place independent	Policy cores	Labor market
Integrality	Selection policy	Programs	Municipalities
Security	Efficiency	Scaling up	Labor force
Standardization	Actor	Collectivity	Employers Unions
Facilities	Effectiveness	Mission/vision assessment	Employee Unions
Information	Predictability	Employer ship	Funds
Maintenance	Planned	Themes and tasks	Other Ministries
Systems	Procedures	Functioning	Independent administrative bodies
Ownership		Organization	Society
Storage			Social and Economic Council
Architecture			Research agencies
			Social partners
			National Archive

5.3   Guiding Statements

To be able to govern the perspectives, and subsequent core concepts, a directional framework is needed consisting of "Guiding Statements" which form an additional class of cohesive elements. We define a guiding statement as: *an internally agreed and published statement which directs desirable behaviour*. Guiding statements may therefore cover policy statements, (normative) principles [33] and objectives. To make the perspectives, including their core concepts, governable, the guiding statements must be assigned to the perspectives and core concepts they pertain to. Some examples of guiding statements are shown in Table 7.

Table 7. Guiding statements relevant to the *processes* perspective

Processes
A dual situation in which paper and digital systems or more systems are used in parallel, should where possible be avoided.
Our organization uses tenet that the entire work of staff and processflow of documents goes digital.
The concept of flexible working means customization (instead of one size fits all).
Existing paper-based processes in our organization are as much as possible adjusted to the features of the automated document management system.
Integral approach: It is important to think about sustainability already at the "front" of the information chain.
Selection policy must play a fully involved role at the beginning of the "information creation".
The coming years it is expected that firm pressure will be on the business operations and IT to operate cost-efficiently.
Working smarter with fewer people.
We aim to ensure the government can operate decisively, transparently and fast.
We involve at the front of the process the external actors in the issues and developments we are working on.
We must have more attention to the process.
In 2012, our work is supported by a modern work environment and we as professionals are equipped to let this environment operate as optimal as possible for us.
We want better performing processes, more efficient and effective.
We want more predictability in our processes.
It must be clear how processes flow through the organization and who has which responsibilities.

5.4   Core Models

To better communicate the directions provided by the guiding statements, it is common to use models to provide more specific instructions. These models provide instructions that represent more specific choices/directions that are consistent with the guiding statements. In other words, these models are in line with the guiding statements formulated for that particular perspective. These models are cohesive elements as well, which we refer to as "Core models". We define a core model as: *a high level view of a perspective, based on and in line with the guiding statements of the corresponding perspective*.

The well known design/engineering frameworks, such as Zachman [32], TOGAF's content framework [7] or the Integrated Architecture Framework [8], have an important role to play in the development of the core models within the different perspectives. Based on their respective underlying "design philosophies", these more design/engineering oriented frameworks provide a way (1) to ensure completeness and consistency from an engineering point of view, (2) to enforce/invite a specific line of reasoning on the design/construction of the enterprise and (3) to classify/structure the different core models. The latter, is also where modelling languages such as ArchiMate [10], e3Value [34], BPMN [35], or UML [36] can be used. Furthermore, frameworks such as Zachman [32], or TOGAF's content framework [7], can be used to further structure the core models within the perspectives.

5.5   Relevant Relationships

The real world case studies conducted within the GEA programme have shown that guiding statements can be allocated pre-dominantly to one perspective, although they often also address other perspectives as well. This means that it is possible that a single guiding statement relates several perspectives and in this way establishes one or more relationships between these perspectives. To clearly connect the perspectives from both ends, while firmly founding these relationships within the involved perspectives, the guiding statements are (re)formulated in terms of the concerns/scope of each of the involved perspectives. Similarly, such relationships may also exist between the core concepts and core models of different perspectives.

These relationships are an important feature in ensuring the coherence between the different perspectives. Therefore, we introduce an additional cohesive element: "Relevant relationship", which we define as *a description of the connection between guiding statements from different perspectives*. The relevant relationships should explain in particular the causal relationship between the guiding statements involved.

By formulating the cohesive elements on the design level, the coherence at this level is made explicit. This is illustrated, and summarized, in (the earlier shown) Figure 1. This diagram also shows nine *example* perspectives. As argued before, the actual set of perspectives depends on the organization. Note, that the diagram only aims to put the role of the different cohesive elements in perspective. The diagrams is by no means intended for stakeholder communication.

5.6   Experiences

The presence of a good documented enterprise mission, vision, core values, goals and strategy are preconditions to be able to determine the content of the cohesive elements on the design level of the organization and they are the essential resources for this determination. Case studies with GEA have also shown that GEA makes the relationships between different perspectives of an organization explicit in such a way that it becomes possible to develop integral solutions for important business issues. New and adjusted guiding statements within a perspective will affect other perspectives through the relevant relationships. The insight in the enterprise coherence given by the relevant relationships contributes to the governance of the organization, since the impact of a change in one perspective can be translated into possible effects on the other perspectives. As an example, consider the situation depicted in Figure 3. In this example, "Acquisition", as part of the growth strategy, is a new and important perspective. The main guiding statement in this perspective is: *We acquire only organizations with cutting edge knowledge appropriate to the spearheads of our services*. This statement has implications for other perspectives, primarily for the perspective "Knowledge". In this perspective, due to the new relevant relationship Acquisition/Knowledge, the existing guiding statement: *We innovate our knowledge concepts in line with our service priorities by knowledge CREATION* is adjusted to the guiding statement: *We innovate our knowledge concepts in line with our service priorities by knowledge INTEGRATION*. The relevant relationship responsible for this adjustment is formulated as: "*innovation by buying service concepts*". The change of this guiding statement in the perspective "Knowledge", will subsequently invoke a causal series of first order and even second and higher order changes to guiding statements in other perspectives.

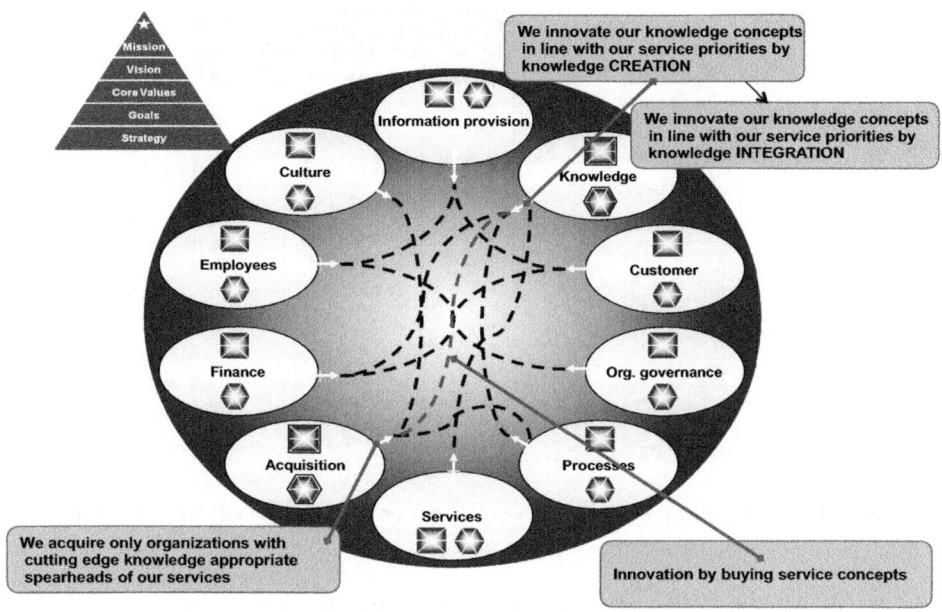

Fig. 3. Example of the working of a relevant relationship

6 Coherence between the Levels

Besides horizontal coherence on one level of contemplation, we also distinguish vertical coherence between two adjacent levels of coherence. To realize the strategic fit, as proposed in the "Strategic Alignment Model" of Henderson & Venkatraman [6], we correlate the cohesive elements defined on the purpose level with the cohesive elements defined on the design level. This has been illustrated in Figure 4.

The fundamental, transcendent, nature of the mission of a company gives a high level understanding of the core activities to excel in, and the desired behaviour. Therefore the enterprise's mission harbours information on relevant perspectives and principles. The guiding statements should therefore also be motivated in terms of the mission. As soon as guiding statements are allocated to different perspectives, enterprise coherence is made explicit by coupling them by means of relevant relationships.

In its vision, an organization elaborates on its envisioned position in the future. Vision statements indicate new candidate perspectives and/or new core concepts. They may also underpin and/or confirm the role of the already identified perspectives and core concepts. Furthermore the envisioned position of the organisation in the future is translated into principles and policy statements. Core values diffuse to the design level by way of principles. These values may also indicate major or minor focus areas to govern, respectively the perspectives and core concepts. Objectives on the design level, defined as a more concrete formulation of an organisation's goal, are derived from the goals on the purpose level. Also goals may indicate major or minor focus areas to govern. Finally the strategy, seen as the strategic execution path to achieve the enterprises

Intensity of coupling Strong ++ Weak +		Core factors on design level						
				Guiding statemts				
		Perspectives	Core concepts	Principles	Objectives	Policy statements	Core models	Relevant relationships
Core factors on the level of meaning	Mission	++		++				++
	Vision	++	+	++		++		++
	Core values	+	+	++				++
	Goals	+	+		++			++
	Strategy	++	++	++	++	++		++

Fig. 4. Correlation between the cohesive elements on two interrelated levels of coherence

goals, supplies the content to major focus areas, the perspectives, minor focus areas, core concepts, and directional information, guiding statements.

In practice there will be many internal and external sources available to gather definitions of the cohesive elements on both the purpose and the design level. As part of the overall governance of enterprise coherence, it is important to continually guard the consistency between these sources and the definitions of the cohesive elements obtained so far. Collectively, the "formal" definitions of the cohesive elements provide the steering instrument which allows senior management to influence enterprise coherence. Different source/documents that deal with the strategy, design, and operations of the enterprise should of course be consistent to the definitions.

In the course of time, several factors may lead to disturbances in already achieved coherence. In such a case, an adjustment in the coherence must be made. An example of such adjustment of a disturbance in the relationship between the level of purpose and the level of design, concerns Philips. During the initial stages of the market for mobile phone, Philips was one of manufacturers of such devices. After some time the dynamics of the selected product×market combination intensified in such a way, that this combination no longer fitted to the definition of Philips' level of purpose. Philips' overall strategy was to operate in slowly circulating markets. However, due to this intensifying dynamics of the mobile phone market, Philips would either have to make fundamental changes at its level of purpose, or make a change to its design level. Philips decided to do the latter, and indeed has withdrawn itself from the mobile phone market.

7   Conclusion and Further Research

In this paper we discussed the Enterprise Cohesion Framework (ECF) as it has been developed iteratively in the multi-client GEA research programme. The framework consists of a number of cohesive elements and relationships expressing the cohesion in an enterprise. As such, it allows enterprise to make their coherence explicit, thus enabling them to govern their coherence. During the development of the framework, members of the GEA research programme applied it to their own organizations. An elaborate discussion of such a case, can be found in [15]. Some insights from these applications include:

- Making enterprise coherence explicit by means of the ECF does indeed require an initial investment, but this investment leads to a clear return on investment in terms of a better understanding of the enterprise's environment, and the coherence in the views among all parties involved.
- When using the ECF operationally, the key players within an organization (i.e. the representatives of the perspectives) do not only get to know and trust each other better, but moreover gain a better insight into and understanding of each other's domains. This means that enterprise coherence is not merely something that takes place in terms of "documents", but actually gets embedded in the social processes among the key players in the enterprise.
- The process of bringing and keeping the key players together in the workshop sessions puts a lot of stress on the required competencies of the facilitators (i.e. the enterprise architects).

In line with the design science rhythm of the GEA programme, we will continue to apply the GEA method in client projects, and based on that further evaluate, extend and improve the GEA method.

References

1. Op't Land, M., Proper, H.A., Waage, M., Cloo, J., Steghuis, C.: Enterprise Architecture – Creating Value by Informed Governance. Enterprise Engineering Series. Springer, Berlin (2008) ISBN-13: 9783540852315
2. Wagter, R.: Sturen op samenhang op basis van GEA – Permanent en event driven. Van Haren Publishing, Zaltbommel (2009) (in Dutch) ISBN-13: 9789087534066
3. Sowa, J.F., Zachman, J.A.: Extending and formalizing the framework for information systems architecture. IBM Systems Journal 31(3), 590–616 (1992)
4. Wagter, R., Van den Berg, M., Luijpers, J., Van Steenbergen, M.: Dynamic Enterprise Architecture: How to Make It Work. Wiley, New York (2005) ISBN-10: 0471682721
5. Abcouwer, A., Maes, R., Truijens, J.: Contouren van een generiek model voor informatie-management. Primavera working paper. Universiteit van Amsterdam (1997) (in Dutch)
6. Henderson, J.C., Venkatraman, N.: Strategic alignment: Leveraging information technology for transforming organizations. IBM Systems Journal 32(1), 4–16 (1993)
7. The Open Group. TOGAF Version 9. Van Haren Publishing, Zaltbommel (2009) ISBN-13: 9789087532307
8. Van't Wout, J., Waage, M., Hartman, H., Stahlecker, M., Hofman, A.: The Integrated Architecture Framework Explained. Springer, Berlin (2010) ISBN-13: 9783642115172
9. Lankhorst, M.M. (ed.): Enterprise Architecture at Work: Modelling, Communication and Analysis. Springer, Berlin (2005) ISBN-10: 3540243712
10. Iacob, M.-E., Jonkers, H., Lankhorst, M.M., Proper, H.A.: ArchiMate 1.0 Specification. The Open Group (2009) ISBN-13: 9789087535025

11. De Caluwé, L., Vermaak, H.: Learning to Change: A Guide for Organization Change Agents. Sage Publications, London (2003) ISBN-10: 9014961587
12. Wagter, R., Nijkamp, G., Proper, H.A.: Overview 1th Phase - General Enterprise Architecturing. White Paper GEA-1, Ordina, Utrecht, The Netherlands (2007) (in Dutch)
13. Hevner, A.R., March, S.T., Park, J., Ram, S.: Design Science in Information Systems Research. MIS Quarterly 28, 75–106 (2004)
14. Yin, R.K.: Case Study Research – Design and Methods, 4th edn. Sage Publications (2009) ISBN-13: 9781412960991
15. Wagter, R., Proper, H.A., Witte, D.: Enterprise coherence in the dutch ministry of social affairs and employment. In: Huemer, C., Viscusi, G., Rychkova, I., Andersson, B. (eds.) Proceedings of the 7th International Workshop on Business/IT-Alignment and Interoperability (BUSITAL 2012). LNBIP, Springer, Berlin (2012)
16. Graves, T.: Real Enterprise Architecture: beyond IT to the whole enterprise. Tetradian Books, Colchester (2008), http://tetradianbooks.com ISBN-13: 9781906681005
17. Hoogervorst, J.A.P.: Enterprise Governance and Enterprise Engineering. Springer, Berlin (2009) ISBN-13: 9783540926702
18. Fehskens, L.: Deriving Execution from Strategy: Architecture and the Enterprise. In: Open Group Conference Amsterdam. The Open Group (October 2010)
19. Wagter, R., Proper, H.A(E.), Witte, D.: Enterprise coherence assessment version. In: Harmsen, F., Grahlmann, K., Proper, E. (eds.) PRET 2011. LNBIP, vol. 89, pp. 28–52. Springer, Heidelberg (2011) ISBN-13: 9783642233876
20. Lessen uit ICT-projecten bij de overheid, Deel B. De Algemene Rekenkamer (2008), (in Dutch), http://www.rekenkamer.nl/Actueel/Onderzoeksrapporten/Introducties/2008/07/Lessen_uit_ICT_projecten_bij_de_overheid_Deel_B
21. Simons, R.: Levers of Control: How Managers Use Control Systems to Drive Strategic Renewal. Harvard Business School Press (1994) ISBN-13: 9780875845593
22. De Leeuw, A.C.J.: Organisaties: Management, Analyse, Ontwikkeling en Verandering, een systeem visie, Van Gorcum, Assen, The Netherlands (1982) (in Dutch) ISBN-13: 9023222474
23. De Leeuw, A.C.J., Volberda, H.W.: On the Concept of Flexibility: A Dual Control Perspective. Omega, International Journal of Management Science 24(2), 121–139 (1996)
24. Balogun, J., Hope Hailey, V., Johnson, G., Scholes, K.: Exploring Strategic Change, 2nd edn. Financial Times Prent.Int (2003) ISBN-13: 9780273683278
25. Reitsma, E., Jansen, P., Van der Werf, E., Van den Steenhoven, H.: Wat is de beste veranderaanpak? In: Management Executive (July/August 2004) (in Dutch)
26. Kaplan, R.S., Norton, D.P., Barrows, E.A.: Developing the Strategy: Vision, Value Gaps, and Analysis. Balanced Scorecard Review (January-February 2008)
27. Thenmozhi, M.: Module 9 - Strategic Management. Lecture Notes, Department of Management Studies. Indian Institute of Technology Madras, India (2009)
28. Collins, J., Porras, J.: Building Your Company's Vision. Harvard Business Review (1996)
29. Senge, P.M.: The Fifth Discipline – The art and practice of the learning organization. Doubleday, New York (1990) ISBN-13: 9780385517256
30. Chandler, A.D.: Strategy and Structure, Chapters in the History of the American Industrial Enterprise. The MIT Press, Cambridge (1969) ISBN-10: 0262530090
31. The Architecture Working Group of the Software Engineering Committee. Recommended Practice for Architectural Description of Software Intensive Systems. Technical Report IEEE P1471:2000, ISO/IEC 42010:2007, Standards Department. IEEE, Piscataway (September 2000) ISBN-10: 0738125180

32. Zachman, J.A.: A framework for information systems architecture. IBM Systems Journal 26(3) (1987)
33. Greefhorst, D., Proper, H.A.: Architecture Principles – The Cornerstones of Enterprise Architecture. Enterprise Engineering Series. Springer, Berlin (2011),
    http://www.springer.com/business+%26+management/
    business+information+systems/book/978-3-642-20278-0
    ISBN-13: 9783642202780
34. Gordijn, J., Akkermans, H.: Value based requirements engineering: Exploring innovative e-commerce ideas. Requirements Engineering Journal 8(2), 114–134 (2003), doi:10.1007/s00766-003-0169-x
35. Business process modeling notation, v1.1. OMG Available Specification OMG Document Number: formal/2008-01-17, Object Management Group (January 2008)
36. UML 2.0 Superstructure Specification – Final Adopted Specification. Technical Report ptc/03–08–02, OMG (August 2003)

Measuring and Evaluating Business-IT Alignment for RAD Projects Using the REFINTO Framework and Tool

Emem Umoh, Pedro R. Falcone Sampaio, and Babis Theodoulidis

Manchester Business School, University of Manchester
Booth Street East, M15 6PB
Manchester, United Kingdom
emem.umoh@postgrad.mbs.ac.uk,
{p.sampaio,b.theodoulidis}@manchester.ac.uk

Abstract. REFINTO is a requirement engineering framework and tool aimed at facilitating business-IT alignment by using functional and non-functional domain ontologies to guide the rapid application development (RAD) process in financial service software development. In this paper we present the REFINTO measurement and evaluation mechanism for assessing alignment at the tactical and operational levels leveraging the REFINTO framework and tool. The mechanism is based on the Balanced Scorecard and Strategic Alignment Maturity Model. The mechanism offers an innovative and practical method of measuring alignment on a more granular level – per project basis – rather than on high level strategic indicators that often fail to identify and assess the contribution of alignment factors with accuracy. The research described in this paper has been applied to support RAD projects in a top 5 investment bank helping minimize business-IT misalignment prevalent in the RE stage of RAD projects resulting in shorter IT application service delivery times and enhanced quality of IT applications.

Keywords: Rapid Application Development, Requirement Engineering, Business-IT Alignment, Ontology, Balanced Scorecard. Alignment Measurement and Evaluation.

1 Introduction

Obtaining maximum value for large scale investments in IT (return on investment, ROI) remains the main key performance indicator for CIOs and the main challenge to meeting this objective has been consistently identified as misalignment between business and IT within an organization (see [2], [3], [4], and [5]). The cost of misalignment between business and IT can be enormous, including: technology artifacts that are not fit for purpose resulting in resource wastage [6], reputational loss, competitive disadvantages due to inferior systems and services [7], loss of client

E. Proper et al. (Eds.): PRET 2012, LNBIP 120, pp 96–119, 2012.
© Springer-Verlag Berlin Heidelberg 2012

goodwill and market share. Business-IT alignment (BIA) can be briefly defined as the degree to which the IT applications, infrastructure, and organization, enable and support the business strategy and processes of an organization [8]. According to [9], the BIA problem can be approached from three perspectives: architecture, governance and communication. The REFINTO project [1] comprising an ontology-based framework and a semantically-enabled requirements engineering tool was conceptualized to address business-IT alignment issues such as but not limited to 'language-gap' and the 'knowledge-gap' between business and IT stakeholders participating in the requirements engineering process for rapid application development (RAD) projects in a fast moving services industry – the financial services. The framework is currently being applied at a top investment bank for business critical RAD projects. In [1], we discuss the approaches to addressing the BIA problem in detail and provide the rationale for tackling the BIA problem through the communication approach using REFINTO. We have also observed that due to the large vocabulary of business terms and specialized body of knowledge within the financial services industry and its fast moving nature, the communication gap between business and technology teams is even more pronounced. Latest requirements engineering research [19] also indicates that the lack of support for socio-technical factors – in particular, methods and knowledge-based techniques to model social relationships and support social communication between stakeholders – are fundamental limitations of requirements engineering approaches.

In this paper, we address the issue of measuring and evaluating alignment success resulting from the application of our proposed framework and tool in RAD application projects in a top global financial services organization. The importance of being able to measure business and IT alignment cannot be overemphasized. To develop the evaluation and measurement method incorporated to the REFINTO framework we have used as foundations methods, techniques and theories arising from the domain of business requirements quality evaluation, balanced scorecard [10], the strategic alignment maturity model [8],[11],[12], ontology evaluation, software quality measurement and project evaluation methods. These foundational constructs are applied at different stages of the RAD project lifecycle to provide a mechanism for gauging the business-IT alignment achieved and perception of quality of service provided to the business from the perspective of the business. To validate the impact of the proposed framework/tool in delivering better project outcomes we compare projects conceptualized and implemented with the guidance of the REFINTO framework/tool against those implemented without the framework and tool highlighting the benefits of the proposed approach.

The research described in this paper adopted the design research method and its key stages as discussed in [30]: awareness of the problem, suggestions to tackle core issues (hypothesis), artifact development, and artifact evaluation. Following the research method steps, we highlight the BIA problem in RAD projects, propose a framework and tool for guiding the requirements engineering stage of these projects and perform evaluation of this framework and tool. We discuss the requirements and objectives of the framework and illustrate its processes and how it is used in practice. This paper focuses mainly on the evaluation of the framework. The remainder of this paper is organized as follows: Section two provides a background description of the REFINTO framework and tool; Section three presents the BIA evaluation approach supported by REFINTO; Section four discusses the data collection and presents a case study including the evaluation of application development scenarios that used REFINTO against those without using the framework and tool. Section five presents related work and section six concludes the paper and discusses future work.

2   REFINTO Framework and Tool: An Overview

This section provides an overview of the REFINTO framework and tool, the core process flow underpinning the framework and the main activities conducted with the guidance of the framework in the context of RAD projects. We also highlight what is measured at the different stages of RAD projects. The main objective of the REFINTO framework (please refer to [1] for a comprehensive description) is to facilitate a structured approach to requirements engineering for RAD projects in financial services. This systematic approach should result in a more consistent and positive outcome than would be obtained from an ad-hoc process which can be chaotic in a fast moving environment. REFINTO is conceptualized to make the requirements engineering stage of RAD projects more inclusive, reduce the misunderstanding between the business and technology teams due to terminology and process gaps and its attendant effect on project outcomes. This leads to mutual understanding of the perspectives of the project stakeholders. It can also be used to track the progress of projects, making the process of delivering RAD solutions more transparent by giving the business increased visibility of RAD processes. The design philosophy underpinning the REFINTO framework is based on concepts such as reuse, service-orientation, and agility. Significant time and resource savings can be achieved by reusing requirements, business process knowledge, and assets (such as web services, databases, source code, etc.), captured from previous closely related requirements. It can also lead to the extension and improvement of existing processes and assets. With service-orientation techniques incorporated into REFINTO, solutions are built with reuse in mind, making assets self-contained and exposing interfaces to services provided. This facilitates searching, discovering, composing other services from core services. The framework also facilitates agility with support for frequently changing requirements, allowing necessary adjustments to be made and providing visibility on potential effects on project timescales. The REFINTO framework helps to facilitate business-IT alignment at the tactical/operational levels (bottom-top) approach to alignment. There are few practical applications of top-down approaches (at the strategic) level as highlighted in [20] and [21].

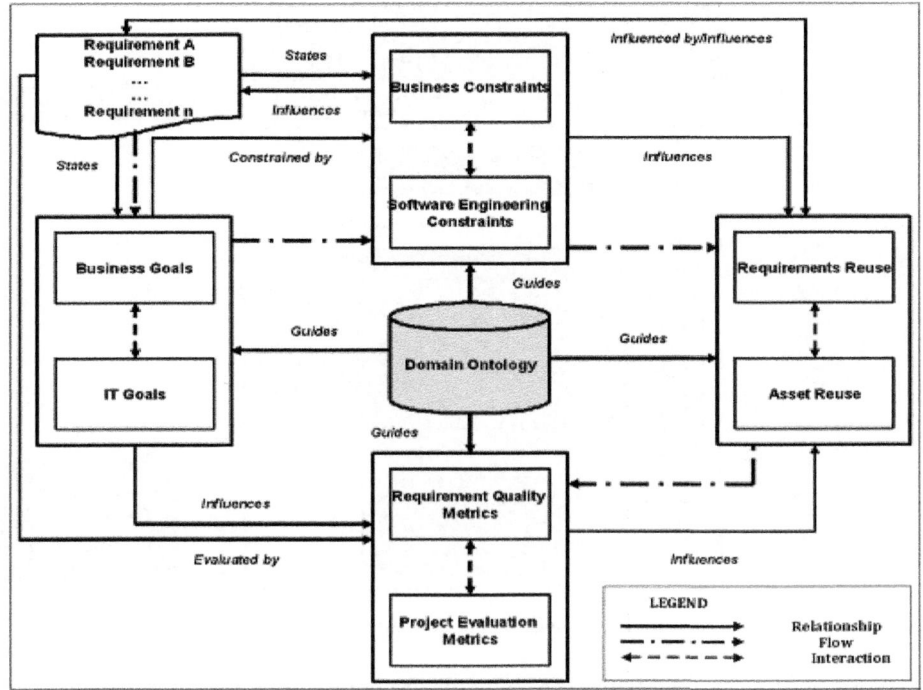

Fig. 1. REFINTO Framework

To use the framework, illustrated in Figure 1, the requirements document which contains both functional and non-functional requirements is the starting point. Stakeholders including subject matter experts, business analysts, requirement engineers, software engineers, and developers determine the initial set of requirements and try to gain an understanding of what is required to meet the business need.

2.1   Architecture of the REFINTO Tool

The REFINTO tool illustrated in Fig. 2 is built on n-tier architecture and implemented in JESS (Java Expert System Shell), using Java for the graphic user interface and control program. Jess Rules (integrated via JessTab) is also used and allows for conflict resolution. It also provides interface for using Protégé knowledge bases. It is semi-automated towards enabling discovery of assets, reasoning about alignment conflicts and inconsistencies across requirements. The main tool components supporting the framework are: the Knowledge-Base, the Inference Engine, and the Control Program described in [1]. The control program includes the Parser, the GUI, libraries, methods and functions that are used to support interaction with stakeholders. The domain, task and functional application ontology in the framework includes those built for reconciliation, external reference data sourcing and external reporting.

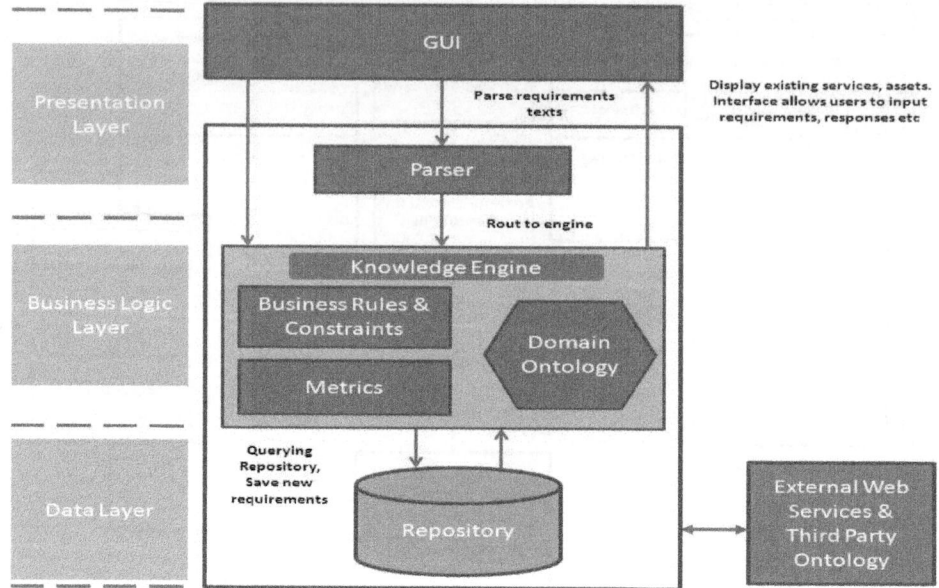

Fig. 2. REFINTO Tool Architecture

Vertical domain ontologies are also incorporated into the tool. A Financial Ontology [26] for example has a rich set of financial services concepts which can be leveraged by the REFINTO tool for projects with relevant scope.

2.2   Using the REFINTO Framework

The REFINTO framework is used throughout the RAD project. Stakeholders have collaborative as well as distinctive roles depending on the stage of the RAD project. To aid clarity and understanding, the process flow diagram of using REFINTO is presented in Figure 3. The entry point of the framework is when initial project requirements described in word documents, excel spreadsheets or text-based e-mails are received by the development team. This must state at a minimum the input, process, and expected output of the project. The initial requirements are written by the business (end users) and typically lack the detail and conciseness that would be expected of requirements that are authored by trained and experienced business analysts. It is worth nothing that although the agile/RAD development methodology does not assume a complete collection of all requirements prior to project initiation as is the practice in the waterfall approach, the methods used at the elicitation stage of requirements engineering are also used in agile/RAD [31]. The unique feature in the agile/RAD methodology is that it allows for requirements variability and evolution. The REFINTO framework supports requirements variability and evolution simply by iteration through the process when requirements are added or changed.

Project initiation sessions are held prior to the start of the RAD project. The business users, project manager and RAD developers attend these sessions. Using

REFINTO framework the RAD solution requested in the initial requirements document is classified into categories for which ontologies have been developed. The ontologies contain what is expected for the respective classification of projects. The main project categories for RAD projects in financial services supported by REFINTO are: reconciliation, reporting, reference data validation, and pricing. An example of reconciliation ontology is presented in [1]. The framework and tool are extensible towards projects falling outside the scope of the current ontologies supported. Some projects fall into more than one category. In these cases the corresponding ontologies are used for the requirements elicitation and refinement through a question and response process between the stakeholders. If there are existing projects of similar goals, classification and of similar context, the requirements and constraints experienced from past projects that may impact meeting the requirements are used to refine the current requirements. This is a collaborative process involving all stakeholders. This process can be performed without tool support. The added advantage of using the tool is to automate the process of parsing the ontology, automating the question response process, and logging of responses. The evaluation of the pre-project processes by all participants indicates their perception of the value of this method of requirements elicitation and how it aligns business users understanding with the RAD developers and vice versa.

The process of finding existing projects of similar classification and context and the creation, extension or reuse of assets (e.g. web service, dynamic link libraries etc) to meet the current requirements is performed by RAD developers. This process in projects executed without the REFINTO framework depends on the best effort of RAD developers. For projects executed with REFINTO framework, RAD developers follow a structured and disciplined process to analyze requirements and reuse or extend existing assets before building new assets. RAD developers following the framework build with reuse in mind. Also the capabilities of new, extended, or reused assets are documented with the new project to guide subsequent projects. The advantage of using tool support at this stage is that it provides RAD developers a WSDL-like directory to ease their task of finding relevant assets to work with. RAD developers can query the repository which contains details of existing assets, automating the process of identifying capabilities for extension or reuse. The evaluation of the 'intra-project' indicates how the requirements elicitation and refinement and the alignment between business and technology achieved in the pre-project might result in the RAD developer identifying, selecting, extending, and reusing appropriate assets to meet the current project's requirements. On completion of the project, 'post-project evaluation' is performed. The participants in the evaluation at this stage are the business users and the project managers. What is evaluated at this stage is that the RAD developers have delivered the right solution for the business users within schedule and cost constraints.

Our hypothesis is that the combination of these three evaluations should give an indication of the business-IT alignment (BIA) achieved for that project. We also hypothesize that when scaled out on a number of projects a reliable measure of BIA at the tactical/operational level of the organization can be obtained. This is expressed in equation (1)

$$\mathbf{B\ (t/o) = (B_a + B_b + \ldots + B_n\ )/n.} \tag{1}$$

Where $B_a \ldots B_n$ are alignment measures on individual projects and B(t/o) is the average alignment at tactical/operational of a set of projects within a specified timeframe.

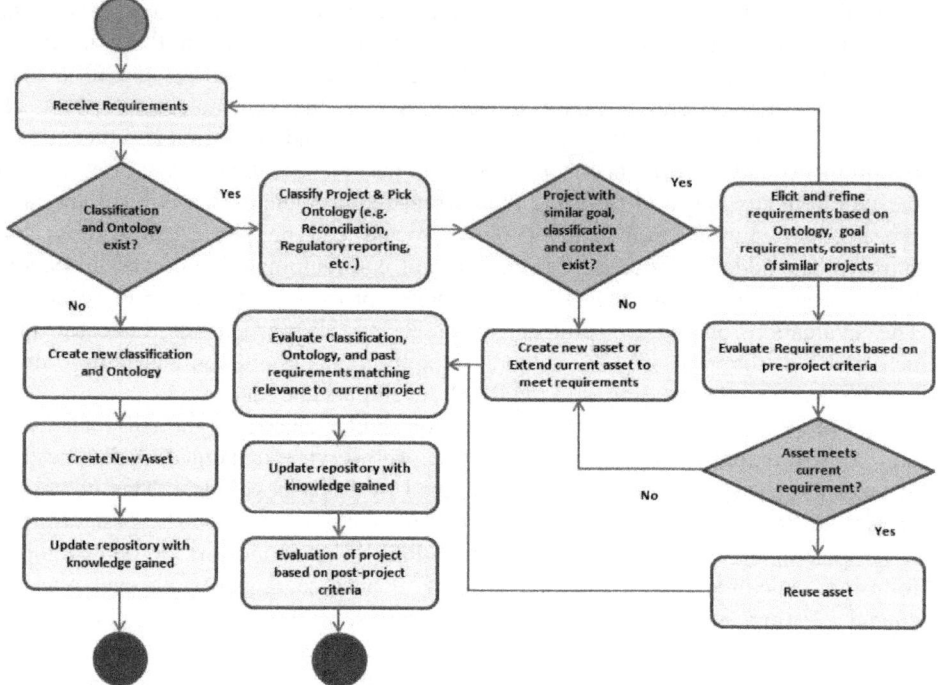

Fig. 3. REFINTO Process Flow Diagram

3   Evaluating BIA Using the REFINTO Framework

The evaluation mechanism of the REFINTO framework is performed through three stages: pre-project, intra-project, and post-project. Figure 4 illustrates the REFINTO project evaluation model. The results of the analysis of projects are then classified according to the levels we have formulated which are closely aligned to the BSC and SAMM models/levels. The main aim of the post-project evaluation survey is to assess the level of alignment attained using the REFINTO framework. Comparing these against projects implemented without the framework should support the hypothesis of the REFINTO framework in measuring business-IT alignment at tactical/operational level for agile/RAD projects. The questions are designed to gauge alignment on the six broad categories of the SAMM model. This research approach has been followed in the following projects ([15],[23], and [24]), but, in our approach, goes further to include questions on the BSC model as well as those relating to requirements quality and project evaluation metrics. A tool to capture and analyze the data has also been developed to support the REFINTO framework. Whereas the SAMM and BSC models are mainly positioned at the strategic level, the REFINTO survey is better suited to the tactical and operation levels where the practical and day to day activities of an organization are carried out. The different stages of the REFINTO alignment evaluation model are now discussed in further details.

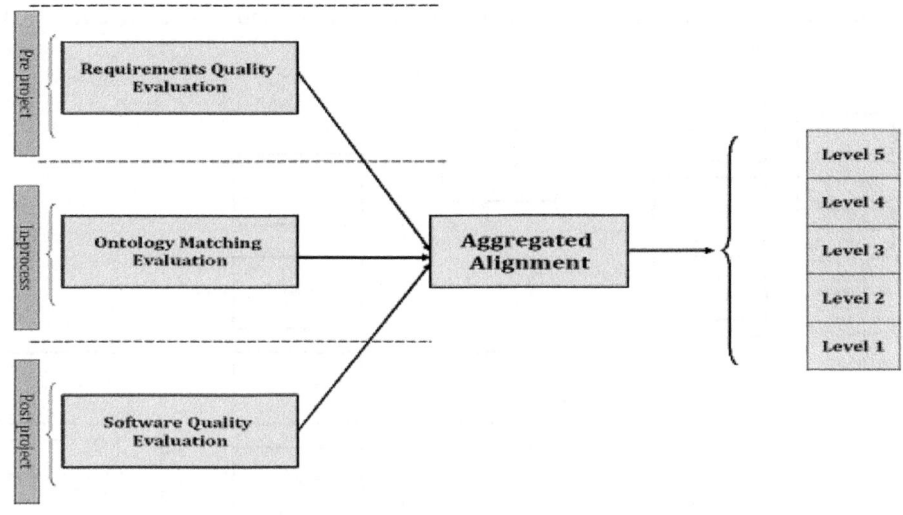

Fig. 4. REFINTO Project Evaluation Model

As earlier stated, the REFINTO framework classification of business-IT alignment perception for projects is designed based on the maturity alignment model SAMM. The metrics are modeled to reflect the BSC perspectives which are learning and growth, business process, customer, and financial perspectives. At the end of a project the participants from the business should have gained knowledge of the RAD processes and RAD developers of the business processes and concepts for which their applications would operate. In the context of REFINTO the business users are the customers.

Figure 5 depicts the scoring process for the different stages of the evaluation. This is analogous to an input-process-output mechanism. The three stages namely pre-project, intra-project and post-projects are evaluated on four points: 'process' (the methods used), learning, savings (financial/time) and communication. Learning indicates the respondents' perspective on the improvement of their understanding of concepts and procedures of the business and technology. Communication indicates transparency of the project stage and if information on progress, issues, and status are readily available and easy to understand. The pre-project evaluation questionnaire is designed to assess requirements quality using research/industry accepted metrics and confirm if there is a positive association between the quality of these requirements and the level of alignment achieved post-project.

The input to the pre-project stage is the respondents' evaluation of the requirements quality, learning, savings (financial/time), and communication through the questionnaire. The scoring starts with assigning a score to a 'sub-process' (e.g. requirements completeness) from 1 to 5. A score of 5 meaning respondent considers the requirements as complete while 1 implies it is incomplete. The score for the requirements quality (process) is the mean score of the sub-processes and is also from 1 to 5, 5 being the highest quality and 1 the lowest quality. The mean score of requirements quality, learning, savings (financial/time) and communication is the score for the pre-project stage.

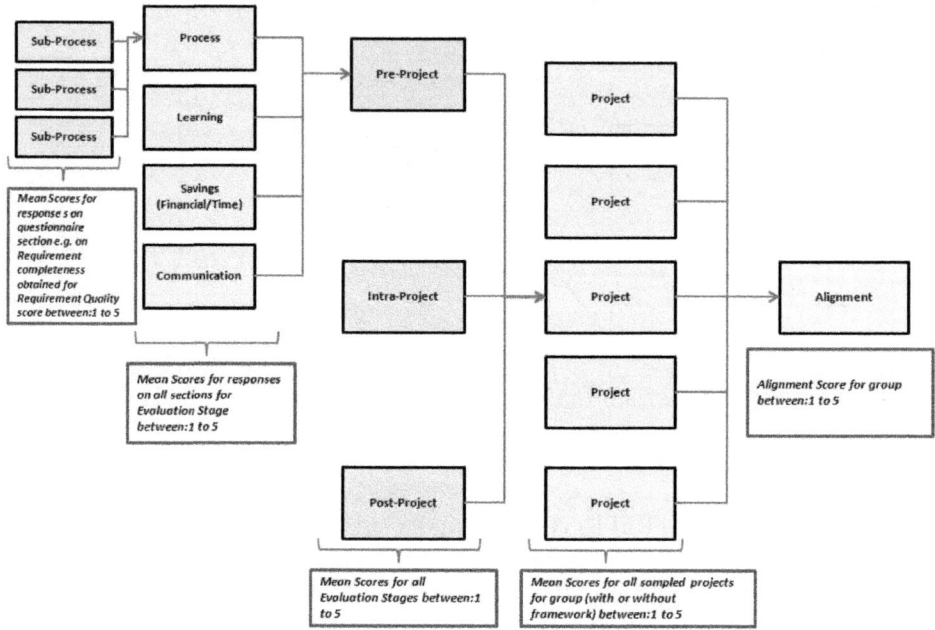

Fig. 5. REFINTO Evaluation Scoring Process

The intra-project evaluation stage involves checks for projects of similar classification and context which, determines if creating new, extending or reusing existing assets (libraries, services, infrastructure, etc) is required to meet current requirements. Respondents evaluate the ease of identification of assets, their relevance to the current requirements, the associated documentation describing the capabilities of the assets. These sub-processes make up the 'process' for the intra-project stage and the mean scores for these sub-processes make up the process score. The mean of the scores for process, learning, saving (financial/time), and communication is the intra-project score.

The post-project evaluation stage involves respondents' evaluating the project based on software estimation and project evaluation measures such as build estimate, staffing, progress, effect of reuse which make up the 'process'. The mean of the scores for these measures and those for learning, saving (financial/time), and communication is the post-project score.

The scores for the three stages of the evaluation can be compared for a set of projects executed with or without the framework and statistical analysis performed to validate the hypothesis put forward in this research. The mean of the pre-project, intra-project, and post-project scores gives the alignment score for that project. The mean score for a group of projects evaluated together is its alignment score.

3.1   Pre-project Evaluation

The pre-project evaluation of the REFINTO framework is focused on the quality of the requirements and the requirements elicitation which is guided by the ontology-based framework and tool. The metrics on which requirements quality is assessed are: lines of texts, imperatives, continuances, weak phrases, completeness, options, directives, and volatility. The quality levels are based on requirements quality metric identified in [27], an analysis of requirements documents from various projects at NASA. The ranking levels are described as follows. Level 1 is the very low quality level. At this level requirements have very high volatility, no directives, incompleteness, no continuances, non optimality of lines of text, mostly weak phrases, too many options leading to ambiguity etc. Level 2 is low quality level and features high volatility, few directives, some incompleteness, few continuances, low optimality of lines of text; weak phrases are common, many options leading to ambiguity etc. At level 3, average quality level, requirements are controlled in some way, directives appear where appropriate, mostly complete/occasional incomplete requirements, continuances appear where appropriate, there is optimality in lines of text, occasional weak phrases, occasional options with potential to cause ambiguity etc. At level 4, high quality level, requirements version control is good with less volatility, incompleteness, no directives; continuances appear where appropriate, optimal lines of text, no weak phrases, where options exist most likely will not cause ambiguity etc. Finally, at level 5, very high quality, excellent control of requirements content and version is established, best practices followed in formulating requirement, directives where appropriate, completeness, optimal lines of text, absolutely no weak phrases, no options leading to ambiguity etc, established elicitation process for business and IT. The pre-project stage evaluation is gauged based on the responses of the participants to questions regarding their perspective of the requirements quality and of the requirement elicitation and refinement process.

3.2   Intra-project Evaluation

The intra-project evaluation stage of the framework focuses mainly on the approach to identifying, selecting, extending or reusing assets. Significant time and cost savings can be made by extending, reusing or modifying existing libraries to meet new requirements. When new requirements for solutions are made to a technology team, there is a tendency to reinvent the wheel. This can lead to longer build time which leads to higher costs. The REFINTO framework aids reuse through the process of classification of requirements and the identification of similar projects of relevant context and the reuse of the assets delivered to meet those requirements. It also requires the documentation of capabilities of the assets and contextual information for the developed assets. Classification of requirements and assets and proper documentation makes it easier to identify and reuse these assets in the future. REFINTO framework ensures this disciplined and systematic approach to creating, maintaining and utilization of inventory is followed. In contrast an ad-hoc approach at this stage as is the case in many RAD projects may result in developers creating assets which may have already been created by another developer or even by the same developer in another project.

The intra-project evaluation involves the respondents evaluating the process of identifying existing assets for reuse or extension and creation if there is no match from existing assets. It also involves their evaluation of the relevance of the assets they have selected for the current requirement and if documentation is available and useful for such assets. This also follows a likert scale of 1 to 5. For example, if a respondent found the identification very useful it would be 5 and if it was found not useful at all it would be assigned a score of 1. These mean scores of these sub-processes of identification, relevance and documentation evaluations is the process score for the intra-project stage. They also evaluate the learning, savings (financial/time) and communication from this stage of the project. The mean score of the process, learning, savings and communication is the score for the intra-project score.

3.3   Post-project Evaluation

The post-project evaluation is aimed at evaluating the perception of the business stakeholders of the deliverables against targets that were agreed to by all stakeholders. The project managers play a critical role towards this evaluation being responsible for reporting project status to business stakeholders. The project manager is also best placed to evaluate on some of the measures of this stage of the REFINTO evaluation model. To avoid bias on the part of the project manager, a different project manager can be furnished with the project details and asked to fill in the questionnaire based on his perception.

The measures for the post-project stage are based on software estimation and project evaluation metrics (see [28], [29]) such as software size (planned and actual number of units, lines of code), staffing (planned and actual levels over time), complexity of each software unit, progress (planned and actual milestones achieved), problems/change status report containing total number of issues, number closed, number opened in the current re-porting period, age and priority. Planned and actual dates for key deliverables and milestones are evaluated. The build release content (planned and actual number of software units released in each build), resource utilization, for example the use of data storage over time against what was specified in the business case is evaluated. The number of items that have been built but have to be scrapped or reworked is also evaluated. For example if a respondent considers the planned and actual dates for key deliverables were exactly as scheduled with no missed deadlines, this will get a score of 5 and if all key deliverables were not delivered as scheduled, this will; receive a score of 1. The respondents evaluate each of these 'sub-processes' and the mean score is the 'process' score for the post-project stage. Respondents also evaluate the learning, savings (time/financial) and communication aspects of the post-project stage. The mean of the scores for the 'process', learning, savings (time/financial) and communication is the score for the post-project stage.

The post-project evaluation scores are very important. Based on our hypothesis the scores at this stage should correlate with the scores from the pre-project and intra-project stages to validate the hypothesis.

4   Data Collection and Analysis

Data collection is through questionnaires filled in by stakeholders involved in the project. The target respondents of the pre-project questionnaires are project managers, developers, and the business users. The questionnaire for the pre-project stage is to gauge the perception of the stakeholders of the requirement elicitation and refinement process and also on the quality and content of the requirements documents against best practices as captured in the requirements quality metrics. The target respondents of the intra-project questionnaires are the developers who have to identify, select, reuse, create or extend assets to meet the requirements. Post-project questionnaires which capture measures that indicate if the project was on schedule and within cost and respondents' perception of the project outcome is targeted at business users and project managers only to avoid bias. The average number of participants per project is 8. Typically this includes 5 from the business, 2 developers and 1 project manager.

The data collection approach adopted involved selection of two sets of 5 RAD projects. One set of 5 projects are executed without the framework/support tool and the other set of 5 projects are executed with the framework/support tool. The main instrument for data collection is the questionnaires administered at the 3 stages of the projects. Emails, bug fix/tracking sheets, interviews with stakeholders, and time reporting sheets used for the projects are also a source of supporting project data. The projects selected for statistical sampling, analysis and evaluation are reflective of the variety from a larger number of projects available for use. Also the detailed analysis performed on each project constrains the sample size to a manageable number of projects. The REFINTO framework is being used on an ongoing basis and in future papers analysis with a much larger dataset will be reported.

4.1   Project Selection for Comparison

The projects selected from those implemented without the REFINTO framework are described in Table 1. Those selected from those implemented with the REFINTO framework are described in Table 2. The domain ontology based classification of each is also provided. The criteria for selecting the projects were similarity in functionality, complexity and size to ensure objectivity in the comparison.

Table 1. Projects Implemented without the REFINTO Framework and Tool

Project	Classification	Description
Project A	External Reference Data, Reconciliation	Requirement for application to retrieve pricing data and compare them to an external reference pricing data service (Bloomberg, Reuters etc)
Project B	External Reference Data, Reconciliation	Requirement for application to select new trades for review based on complex logic and criteria which change frequently
Project C	External Reference Data, Reconciliation, Regulatory Reporting	Requirement for application to select trades for regulatory reporting based on stated criteria and archiving this data monthly
Project D	Reconciliation	Requirement for application to reallocate positions of the same securities held by different legal entities based on complex business processes with potential impact on Profit and Loss.
Project E	External Reference Data, Reconciliation, Regulatory Reporting	Requirement for application to reconcile trades booked in internal trade booking systems against details on the trades in regulator central clearing systems

Table 2. Projects Implemented with the REFINTO Framework and Tool

Project	Classification	Description
Project RA	Regulatory Reporting	Requirement for application for regulatory reporting of trades based on complex business processes based on global reporting regions and large datasets
Project RB	Reconciliation	Requirement for application to select new trades for review irrespective of product with an intelligent retrieval and validation feature
Project RC	External Reference Data, Reconciliation	Requirement for application to identify all pricing data that have not changed in 2 or 5 days, verify with external reference pricing data sources (Bloomberg, Reuters etc) and allow users to affirm or comment on each.
Project RD	Reconciliation, Regulatory Reporting	Requirement for application to reconcile reported trade details from/through different systems up to regulator and validate what regulator receives.
Project RE	Reporting	Requirement for MIS application to report consolidated trade details to management

4.2   Pre-project Analysis

Descriptive statistical analysis performed on the samples at this stage are depicted in Figures 6 and 7 which show the pre-project scores on the items evaluated at that stage of the project. From the scores shown in Figure 6 for projects implemented without the framework and in Figure 7 for those implemented with the framework it can be observed that projects executed with the REFINTO project have higher scores at this stage. A side by side comparison of the numbers shown in Table 3 which shows the mean scores on each of the evaluation metrics for both sets of projects makes the difference clearer.

Table 3. Comparison of Pre-project scores of two samples

Criteria	REFINTO Projects	Non-REFINTO Projects
Lines of Text	3.628	3.04
Imperatives	3.502	2.844
Continuances	3.562	2.828
Directives	3.856	2.83
Weak Phrases	3.762	3.048
Completeness	3.548	2.692
Options	3.888	3.594
Volatility	3.338	2.706
Structure	3.974	2.774
Elicitation Method	3.61	2.462
Learning	3.534	2.292
Savings (Financial/Time)	3.798	2.152
Communication	3.56	1.992

Independent t-tests was performed on these two sets of samples. The result shows that the framework is effective in improving the pre-project stage of the sampled projects.

Table 4. t-Test: Two-Sample Assuming Equal Variances for Pre-project

	REFINTO	NON-REFINTO
Mean	3.6585	2.7118
Variance	0.0332	0.17653
Observations	13	13
Pooled Variance	0.1049	
Hypothesized Mean Difference	0	
df	24	
t Stat	7.4524	
P(T<=t) one-tail	0.000	
t Critical one-tail	1.7109	
P(T<=t) two-tail	0.0000	
t Critical two-tail	2.0639	

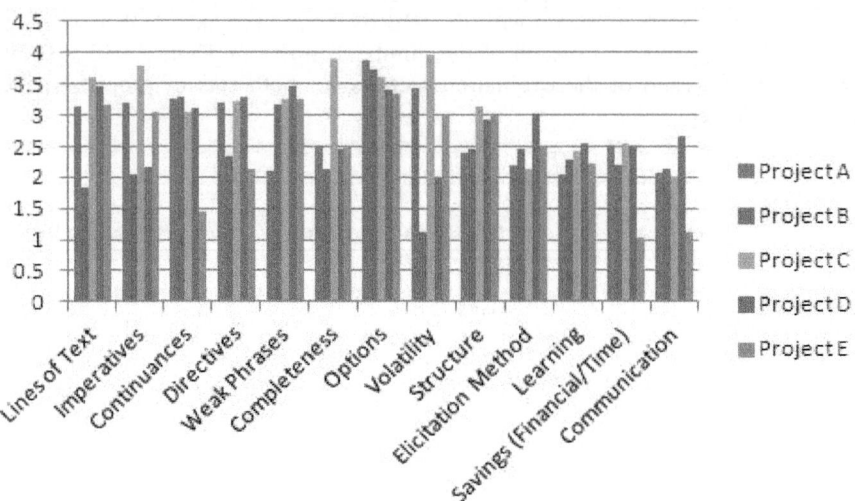

Fig. 6. Pre-project Analysis for Projects not guided by REFINTO

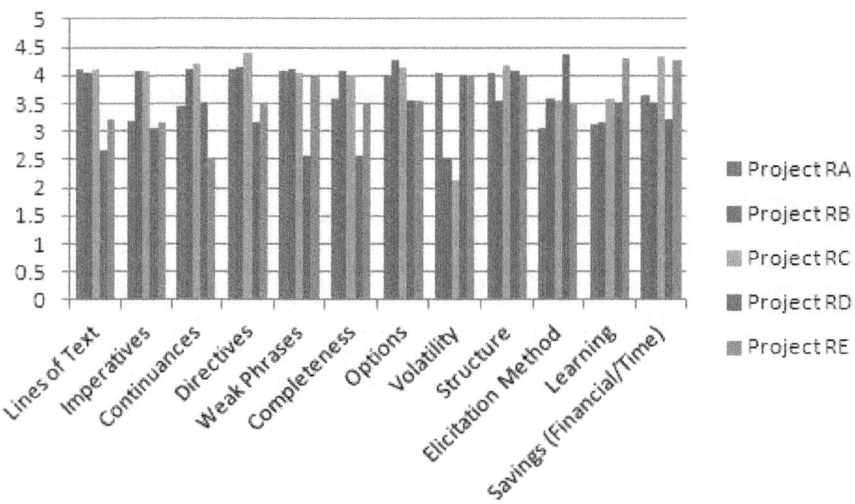

Fig. 7. Pre-project Analysis for Projects guided by REFINTO

4.3   Intra-project Analysis

Descriptive statistical analysis was also performed on the samples at the intra-project stage as depicted in Figures 8 and 9. From the scores shown in Figure 8 for projects implemented without the framework and in Figure 9 for those implemented with the framework it can be observed that projects executed with the REFINTO framework have higher scores at this stage correlating to the scores obtained in the pre-project stage of the sampled projects. A side by side comparison of the numbers is shown in Table 5 which highlights the difference in the mean scores on each of the evaluation metrics for both sets of projects.

Table 5. Comparison of Intra-project scores for two sample sets

Criteria	REFINTO	NON-REFINTO
Identification	3.58	2.046
Documentation	3.75	2.408
Relevance	3.106	1.918
Learning	3.476	2.354
Savings (Financial/Time)	3.26	3.26
Communication	3.734	2.028

Table 6. t-Test: Two-Sample Assuming Equal Variances for Intra-project

	REFINTO	NON-REFINTO
Mean	3.4843	2.1207
Variance	0.0671	0.0430
Observations	6	6
Pooled Variance	0.0550	
Hypothesized Mean Difference	0	
df	10	
t Stat	10.0664	
P(T<=t) one-tail	0	
t Critical one-tail	1.8125	
P(T<=t) two-tail	0.0000	
t Critical two-tail	2.2282	

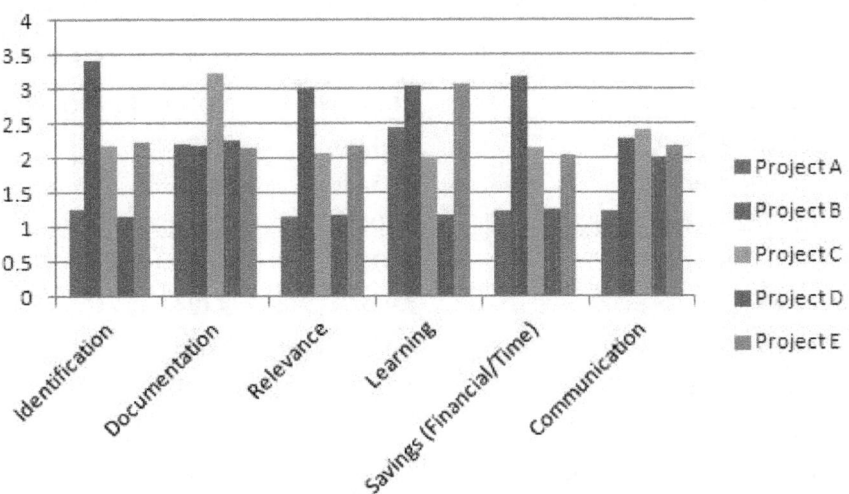

Fig. 8. Intra-project Analysis for projects not guided by REFINTO

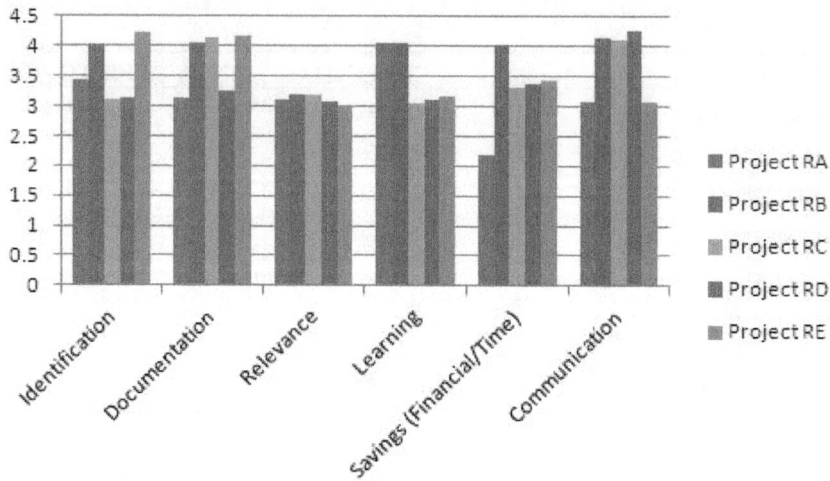

Fig. 9. Intra-project Analysis for projects guided by REFINTO

The independent *t*-tests performed on the intra-project sets of samples shows that the framework is effective in improving the intra-project stage of the sampled projects. This correlates with the *t*-tests performed at the pre-project stage.

4.4   Post-project Analysis

Descriptive statistical analysis as well as t-test were performed on the samples at the post-project stage as depicted in Figures 10 and 11. From the scores shown in Figure 10 for projects implemented without the framework and in Figure 11 for those implemented with the framework it can be observed that projects executed with the REFINTO framework have higher scores at this stage. There is also a correlation between the scores obtained in the pre-project and intra-project stages of the sampled projects. Table 7 which shows the difference in the mean scores on each of the evaluation metrics for both sets of projects.

Table 7. Comparison of Post-project scores for two sample sets

Criteria	REFINTO	NON-REFINTO
Logical Bugs	3.842	2.786
Scrap/Rework	3.654	2.822
Meetings/Workshops	3.104	2.628
Build Estimate	3.372	3.358
Staffing	3.928	3.124
Progress	3.652	2.606
Effect of Reuse	3.7	3.138
Learning	3.604	2.24
Savings (Financial/Time)	3.764	1.648
Communication	3.438	2.328

Table 8. t-Test: Two-Sample Assuming Equal Variances for Post-project

	REFINTO	*NON-REFINTO*
Mean	3.6058	2.6678
Variance	0.0592	0.2541
Observations	10	10
Pooled Variance	0.1567	
Hypothesized Mean Difference	0	
df	18	
t Stat	5.2993	
P(T<=t) one-tail	0.0000	
t Critical one-tail	1.7341	
P(T<=t) two-tail	0.0000	
t Critical two-tail	2.1009	

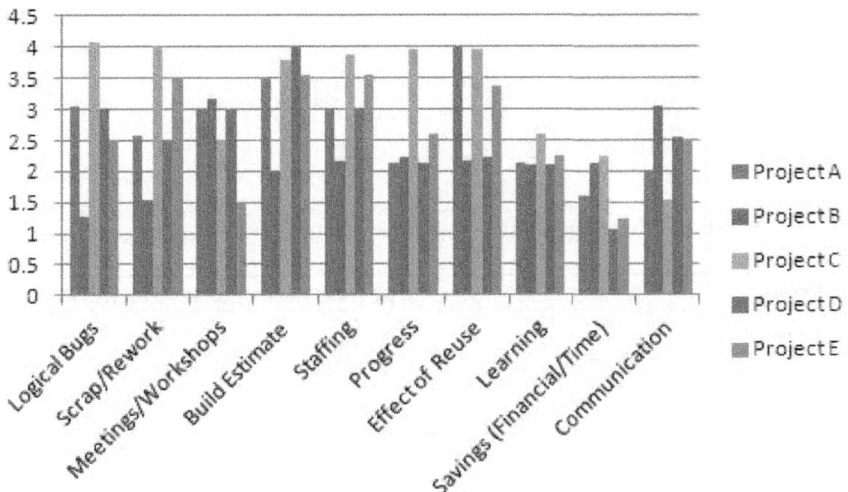

Fig. 10. Post-project Analysis for projects not guided by REFINTO

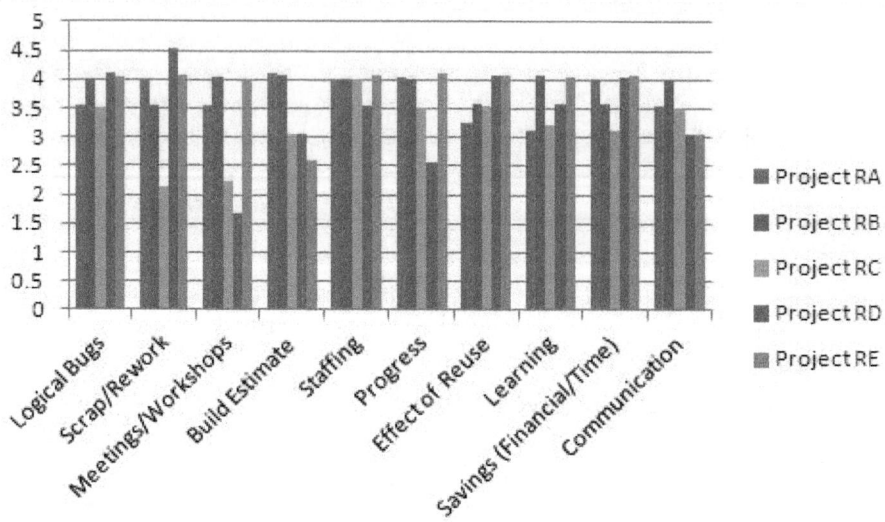

Fig. 11. Post-project Analysis for projects guided by REFINTO

The independent *t*-tests performed on the post-project sets of samples shows that the framework is effective in improving the post-project stage of the sampled projects. This is in line with the *t*-tests scores at the pre-project stage and the intra-project stages of the sample sets.

A combination of the mean scores at the pre-project, intra-project and post-projects evaluation scores also validate the scores obtained. Table 9 shows the mean scores for these stages for the different stages.

Table 9. Comparison of combined mean scores for two sample sets

Stage	REFINTO	NON-REFINTO
Pre-Project	3.628	2.7119
Intra-Project	3.4843	2.1207
Post-Project	3.6058	2.6678

Linking these scores to the REFINTO evaluation model by normalizing the mean score obtained for the two sets of projects, it is observed that the projects executed with the framework shows an improvement of one notch up the scale. Depending on whether the scores from both sample sets are scaled up or down, the alignment obtained from REFINTO guided projects indicate an improvement of a level better than those executed without the framework.

Table 10. t-Test: Two-Sample Assuming Equal Variances for all stages

	REFINTO	*NON-REFINTO*
Mean	3.5727	2.5001
Variance	0.0060	0.1085
Observations	3	3
Pooled Variance	0.0572	
Hypothesized Mean Difference	0	
df	4	
t Stat	5.4916	
P(T<=t) one-tail	0.0027	
t Critical one-tail	2.1319	
P(T<=t) two-tail	0.0054	
t Critical two-tail	2.7765	

4.5   Reflections on Results

In performing the evaluation of the projects that were performed with the guide of the REFINTO framework and those performed without the framework, care was taken to ensure that bias was not introduced into the process. Also efforts were made to ensure that similar projects were selected and the metrics were relevant to both sets of projects. The results as analyzed indicate that the framework has potential to facilitate the improvement of business-IT alignment at a tactical/operation level. The measures applied in this evaluation relate back to the SAMM and BSC models. The learning and savings metrics are adapted from the BSC model. The communication measure is from SAMM. The final mapping of the evaluation measure is against the SAMM. The measure 'staffing' for instance can be quantified in terms of FTE (full time employee) savings. This is a financial measure. Scrap/rework also relates to FTE cost or savings. On the questionnaire (post-project), there are questions relating to the level of visibility of the requirements engineering process that stakeholders on the business and IT had for example on the impact changes to requirements or software engineering constraints had. This relates to the communication and partnership measures in the SAMM model.

In some of the projects that were implemented with the guide of the REFINTO framework there were lower scores than envisaged. This brings to fore the importance of human factors and the effects of building applications with for evolving business processes and the peculiar nature of RAD/Agile projects.

Having obtained a medium for measuring business-IT alignment at the tactical/operational level it is worth considering how idea, concepts and experience gained from applying the REFINTO framework can be applied in an enterprise scale and if it would scale. As discussed in the limitations section of the paper agile/RAD teams/projects are typically set up as small teams to ensure interaction between business and IT. However as agile/RAD and business teams within the enterprise adopt the framework and approach it should have an accumulative effect of improving business-IT alignment.

Practitioners will find the REFINTO framework useful in improving business-IT alignment at a tactical/operational level in their organizations. Adopting the REFINTO framework gives the business participants in the RAD projects opportunities to interact more closely with the RAD developers and project managers. It makes them realize the importance of clearly defining their requirements. The link between requirements quality, elicitation method and the outcome of projects reinforces this. The learning and communication aspects emphasized in the framework ensure that participants in the project gain an understanding of the concepts from the business and technology. The time and cost savings gained from a disciplined and structured approach as well as emphasis on reuse will also proof to be useful to practitioners.

4.6   Limitations of the REFINTO Evaluation Mechanism

A limitation and drawback of the REFINTO evaluation mechanism is that it is difficult to objectively compare the intra-process evaluation of the REFINTO guided projects to projects that are executed without the framework. This can be attributed to the challenges of attempting to evaluate the thought process or way of working of RAD developers not using the framework and comparing this to the more structured disciplined and prescriptive nature of the REFINTO guided processes.

Another limitation of the REFINTO framework and the evaluation mechanism is the relatively small size of participants per project. However this is inherently a limitation with agile/RAD projects. The essence is to keep both IT and business teams to a small number to enhance interaction [31].

Executing a set of projects with a similar business-IT alignment evaluation framework other than REFINTO and performing a comparison/analysis between REFINTO-guided approach and the chosen framework would further validate the REFINTO framework evaluation mechanism. These limitations and further validation of the REFINTO evaluation framework will be performed and reported in a subsequent paper.

5   Related Work

Business-IT Alignment has been measured using variants of Strategic Alignment Maturity Model (SAMM) and Balanced Scorecard (BSC) independently in previous works. To the best of our knowledge there is no existing work that takes the approach of combining components of these two methods in addition to other metrics such as requirements quality, ontology evaluation and post project evaluation metrics to measure business-IT alignment. A brief overview of work related to business-IT alignment measurement is now necessary.

A simple instrument to measure BIA maturity is presented in [15]. It is based solely on the SAMM. It focuses on providing a high-level view of alignment maturity for upper level management. The instrument for collecting data is a survey, which took into consideration the roles of the respondents. The questionnaires covered each of the six components of SAMM. Responses were then analyzed on the six components and graphical representations produced to depict alignment on the 5 scales of SAMM. In [13], a method using BSC to measure and modify IT governance in healthcare organizations is proposed. The authors' argue that using BSC as the sole tool by the organization and its IT department to measure performance facilitates using a common language with benefits for standardization and coordinated approach to BIA. For data collection they also use questionnaires. In [14] a review of the effectiveness of a variant of BSC adapted by a pharmaceutical company compares to the SAMM and BSC. The company under review has multiple businesses each with its corresponding IT departments with different strategies. For each of the business line, a business line BSC is developed. Also for each of the IT departments facing up to the businesses IT BSCs are also developed. The pairs of IT and business line BSCs are then cascaded for the purpose of strategy and objectives alignment measurement unveiling varied levels of alignment in the company. In [4], using a case study research approach, the phenomenon of the IT BSC and its development and implementation in a single organization is investigated at a Canadian financial institution. It provides a guide for building an IT BSC and for linking to organizational objectives. A meta-model for business-IT alignment is proposed is [22].

6   Conclusions and Future Work

This paper proposes an evaluation and measurement mechanism for REFINTO an ontology-based framework and tool to guide the requirements engineering process in RAD projects for financial solution application development. The mechanism demonstrated high potential for facilitating alignment assessment at tactical and operational levels which represent valid baselines for predicting strategic alignment if independent alignment measures are consolidated to give a more holistic view. The approach taken in the REFINTO framework combines techniques from SAMM and BSC and the three-pronged evaluation process is innovative and strengthens the value of the REFINTO framework in facilitating mutual understanding between business and IT stakeholders during the requirements engineering process. The advantages accruing to financial services organizations will include streamlined requirements engineering process for RAD projects, reduction in requirements ambiguity, bridging the language barrier, and ensuring business and IT agree on what should be built. The evaluation and measurement mechanism was validated through case studies verifying the benefits of the framework in facilitating business-IT alignment in RAD projects conducted in a large financial services organization. Future work will be on context-awareness of the REFINTO framework service querying, discovery, and composition. Further validation of the framework continues with more projects implemented with and without guidance from the framework and tool.

References

1. Umoh, E., Sampaio, P., Theodoulidis, B.: REFINTO: An ontology-based requirements engineering framework for business-IT alignment in financial services organizations. In: 9th IEEE Conference on Service Computing, pp. 600–607. IEEE Press (2011)
2. Chan, Y.: Why Haven't We Mastered Alignment? The importance of the Informal Organization Structure. MIS Quarterly Executive 1, 97–112 (2002)
3. Grembergen, W., Haes, S., Brempt, H.: Prioritizing and Linking Business and IT Goals in the Financial Sector. In: 40th Hawaii International Conference on System Science, p. 235a. IEEE Press, Waikoloa (2007)
4. Grembergen, W., Saull, R., Haes, S.: Linking the IT Balanced Scorecard to the Business Objectives at a Major Canadian Financial Group. J. Info. Tech. Cases and Application (2003)
5. Haes, S., Grembergen, W.: Practices in IT Governance and Business/IT Alignment. J. Information Systems Control 2, 1–6 (2008)
6. Baida, Z., Gordijn, J., Omelayenko, B., Akkermans, H.: A Shared Service Terminology for Online Service Provisioning. In: 6th International Conference on Electronic Commerce, pp. 1–10. ACM, Delft (2004)
7. Ralha, C., Gostinski, R.: A Methodological Framework for Business-IT Alignment. In: IEEE/IFIP International Workshop, pp. 1–10. IEEE Press, Salvador (2008)
8. Silvius, A.: Exploring Differences in the Perception of Business & IT Alignment. Communications of the IIMA 7, 21–32 (2007)
9. Chen, H.: Towards Service Engineering: Service Orientation and Business-IT Alignment. In: Hawaii International Conference on System Science. IEEE Press (2008)
10. Kaplan, R., Norton, D.: The Balanced Scorecard: Translating Strategy into Action. Harvard Business School Press, Boston (1996)
11. Luftman, J.: Assessing Business-IT Alignment Maturity. Communications of AIS 4, 1–50 (2004)
12. Luftman, J.: Measure Your Business-IT Alignment. Optimize: Business execution for CIOs Magazine (26) (December 2003)
13. Borousan, E., Hojabri, R., Manafi, M., Hooman, A.: Balanced Scorecard: a Tool for Measuring and Modifying IT Governance in Healthcare Organizations. International Journal of Innovation, Management and Technology 2, 141–146 (2011)
14. Bricknall, R., Darrell, G., Nilsson, H., Pessi, K.: Aligning IT Strategy with Business Strategy through the Balanced Scorecard in a Multinational Pharmaceutical Company. In: 40th Annual Hawaii International Conference on System Sciences, Hawaii (2007)
15. Khaiata, M., Zualkernan, I.: A Simple Instrument to Measure IT-Business Alignment. Information Systems Management 26, 138–152 (2009)
16. Brank, J., Grobelnik, M., Mlaadenic, D.: A Survey of Ontology Evaluation Techniques. In: 11th Conference on Data Mining and Data Warehouses, pp. 166–170. ACM, Chicago (2005)
17. Tartir, S., Arpinar, I., Sheth, A.: Ontological Evaluation and Validation. In: Theory and Applications of Ontology (TAO), vol. 2. Springer, Berlin (2008)
18. Tartir, S., Arpinar, I.: Ontology Evaluation and Ranking using OntoQA. In: 1st IEEE International Conference on Semantic Computing, pp. 185–192. IEEE Press, Irvine (2007)
19. Yu, E., Giorgini, P., Maiden, N., Mylopoulos, J.: Social Modeling for Requirements Engineering. MIT Press (2011)

20. Bleisten, S., Cox, K., Verner, J.: Validating Strategic Alignment of Organizational IT Requirements Using Goal Modeling and Problem Diagrams. The Journal of Systems and Software 79, 362–378 (2006)
21. Guitierrez, A., Orozco, J., Serrano, A.: Factors Affecting IT and Business alignment: A Comparative Study in SMEs and Large Organizations. J. of Enterprise Information Management 22, 197–210 (2009)
22. Plazaola, L., Molina, E., Vargas, N., Flores, J., Ekstedt, M.: A Metamodel for Strategic Business and IT Alignment Assessment. In: 4th Conference on Systems Engineering Research, California (2006)
23. Guitierrez, A., Orozco, J., Serrano, A., Serrano, A.: Using tactical and operational factors to assess Strategic Alignment: an SME Study. In: European and Mediterranean Conference on Information Systems, Costa Blanca, Alicante (2006)
24. Chen, L.: Business-IT alignment Maturity of Companies in China. Information & Management 47, 9–16 (2010)
25. Omoronyia, I., Sindre, G., Stålhane, T., Biffl, S., Moser, T., Sunindyo, W.: A Domain Ontology Building Process for Guiding Requirements Elicitation. In: Wieringa, R., Persson, A. (eds.) REFSQ 2010. LNCS, vol. 6182, pp. 188–202. Springer, Heidelberg (2010)
26. Vanderlinden, E.: Finance Ontology (November 30, 2011), http://fadyart.com
27. Rosenberg, L.: Requirements, Testing and Metrics. In: 16th Annual Pacific Northwest Software Quality Conference, Portland, pp. 107–122 (1998)
28. Stark, G., Durst, R.: Using Metrics in Management Decision Making. In: Oman, P., Pfleeger, S. (eds.) Applied Software Metrics. IEEE Press, Los Alamitos (1997)
29. Madachy, R.: Software Process Dynamics. John Wiley, New Jersey (2008)
30. Hevner, A., Chatterjee, S.: Design Research in Information Systems- Theory and Practice. Integrated Series in Information Systems 22, 1–8 (2010)
31. Sillitti, A., Succi, G.: Requirements Engineering for Agile Methods. In: Aurum, A., Wohlin, C. (eds.) Engineering and Managing Software Requirements, pp. 309–326. Springer (2005)

Author Index